PLANT BASED

FOR BEGINNERS!

Publications International, Ltd.

Pictured on the front cover: Hummus Veggie Bowl *(page 104).*

Pictured on the back cover *(clockwise from top left):* Fattoush Salad *(page 54),* Greek Salad Bowl with Farro and Chickpeas *(page 114),* Beet and Walnut Burgers *(page 82),* Apple Cranberry Crumble *(page 182),* Pepita Lime Cabbage Slaw *(page 30)* and Marinated Tomato Salad *(page 36).*

Photograph on front cover and page 105 copyright © Shutterstock.com.

ISBN: 978-1-64558-390-5

Manufactured in China.

8 7 6 5 4 3 2 1

Let's get social!

 @Publications_International

 @PublicationsInternational

www.pilbooks.com

CONTENTS

TOFU

Adding more tofu to your diet can help you move away from meat without feeling like there's a huge hole left behind. Cook up a batch using the method below and toss it with barbecue sauce, hot sauce, yuzu, teriyaki, pesto, zhug or any other sauce you're craving. Stuff it in a sandwich, layer it in a bowl, or snack on it throughout the day.

Line a sheet pan with foil or parchment paper and lightly brush with oil. Cut the tofu into cubes or rectangles and spread on the pan. Drizzle with soy sauce or sprinkle with salt and toss to coat. Bake at 400°F for 20 minutes or until crispy, turning once. Or use an air fryer if you have one. Cook the tofu at 375°F for 20 minutes or until the tofu is crispy and browned, stirring occasionally.

WHAT IS PLANT-BASED EATING?

Plant-based eating sounds easy. Base your diet on plants, right? Yes, but if you mention plant-based in a room full of people, it will mean something different to everyone.

Opinions vary widely on the definition, and feelings can be heated. People who regularly include meat in their diet may think plant-based is eating more plants along with meat, and perhaps reducing the amount of meat. Those who are already vegetarian may think it means giving up all meat, dairy and eggs completely, while others may say that true plant-based eating means a diet comprised of exclusively organic, local and sustainable plant products, with no dairy, eggs or refined grains, sugar and oils.

So then what is it? The answer is pretty much up to you and how far you want to go. All of the examples above are acceptable, and you may find that you want to transition from eating meat to being vegetarian, and then maybe vegan.

For the purposes of this book, plant-based is defined as always vegetarian and mostly dairy- and egg-free. The important thing, however, is to focus on eating mostly fruit, vegetables and grains and not to get caught up in labels.

Since you're just starting out, go easy on yourself and make small positive changes. Adjust your diet incrementally so that you're not overwhelmed with big changes all at once. You want to strike a balance between eating enough plants and making yourself crazy. The first step is to eat more plants and begin to think of meat, eggs and dairy products as garnishes instead of center-of-the plate items.

SO WHAT DOES MY PLATE LOOK LIKE WITHOUT MEAT AT THE CENTER?

If you're used to thinking of a meal as a protein, a vegetable and a starch, it can be hard to conceptualize a dinner without these traditional elements filling your plate. You can still have that—it just may not look the same as you're used to. For example, Lentils with Pasta on page 101 contains protein (lentils), vegetables (tomatoes, onions) and starch (pasta). It's all mixed up so it may feel like you're only eating one thing but everything is there. If you need more variety, try serving it with steamed or roasted asparagus, broccoli or cauliflower and toasted French bread.

If your usual dinner is cheesy pasta, start with Lemon Cream Pasta with Roasted Cauliflower on page 110. The creaminess of cheesy pasta is there thanks to a light lemon béchamel sauce with a bit of Parmesan thrown in, but you've upped your dinner game by adding lots of veggies in the form of tender roasted cauliflower and peppery arugula, and protein with almonds.

If your usual dinner is takeout fried rice or pizza, try Thai Veggie Curry on page 128 or Spaghetti with Fresh Tomato-Olive Sauce on page 120 for similar Thai and Italian flavors but with a plantier, healthier spin.

If you eat breakfast, try something easy like Overnight Chia Oat Pudding on page 10. With minimal effort the night before, you'll have breakfast waiting for you when you need it. Hot cereals like steel-cut oats, rice pudding and quinoa reheat very well in the microwave or in a saucepan on the stovetop so they too can be made ahead.

All of these recipes are vegetarian and most are vegan, but you can have meat and dairy in your life if you want it. Add an egg or a bit of chicken to the salads or entrées and you're still getting the benefits of a plant-based diet.

ADD MORE PLANTS TO YOUR DAY

Even on days when you're not up for making a five-part bowl recipe or chopping for a salad, you can still easily add vegetables. You can roast just about any vegetable you can think of, and then top with a sauce (chimichurri, pesto, marinara), serve over pasta or tuck into tortillas with salsa for the best tacos. Preheat your oven to 400°F and cut the vegetables into pieces (wedges, cubes, sticks) or leave whole. Toss with olive oil, salt and pepper, and any other seasonings you'd like and spread on a sheet pan. Roast for 20 minutes. Check at this point; some vegetables like carrots may be done. Otherwise, stir the vegetables and add another 10 minutes. Keep checking and stirring until they're as browned and tender as you'd like.

EAT CLEAN

If you're eating a plant-based diet, you may want to incorporate some clean eating strategies as well.

- Eat foods in their natural state (or as close as possible).

- Avoid processed foods, refined sugars (white sugar) and refined grains (white flour).

- Plan your meals and go shopping with a list. This way you'll be less tempted by unhealthy foods.

- Go through your pantry and get rid of anything old, stale or processed. You'll start fresh and know what you have.

- Stock up on canned beans, tomatoes, water-packed fruit, brown rice, whole wheat pasta, olive oil and frozen veggies. A quick and healthy plant-based meal will be at the ready and you'll feel less tempted to make unhealthy choices.

BREAKFAST

LEMON BLUEBERRY OATMEAL
MAKES 4 SERVINGS

1. Melt butter in large saucepan over medium-high heat. Add oats; cook about 6 minutes or until oats are browned and fragrant, stirring frequently. Stir in water and salt; mix well. Reduce heat to medium-low; simmer 15 to 20 minutes or until oats are tender, stirring occasionally.

2. Meanwhile, grate 4 teaspoons peel from lemons; squeeze 3 tablespoons juice.

3. Stir lemon juice, 2 teaspoons grated peel and 2 tablespoons honey into oats. Scoop into bowls. Top each serving with blueberries, almonds and remaining lemon peel; drizzle with remaining honey.

2 tablespoons vegan plant butter or regular butter

$1\frac{1}{4}$ cups steel-cut oats

$3\frac{3}{4}$ cups water

$\frac{1}{2}$ teaspoon salt

2 lemons

4 tablespoons honey, divided

$\frac{3}{4}$ cup fresh blueberries

$\frac{1}{2}$ cup chopped toasted almonds*

*To toast almonds, cook in small skillet over medium heat about 5 minutes or until lightly browned and fragrant, stirring frequently.

MIXED POTATO LATKES

MAKES 10 LATKES

1. Cut potatoes in half; cut into ribbons with thin ribbon blade of spiralizer. Pile loosely on cutting board; cut three times as if cutting into six wedges.* Place potatoes and shallot in large bowl.

2. Whisk eggs, flour, salt, baking powder and nutmeg in small bowl. Add to potatoes; mix until well blended.

3. Heat oil in large skillet over medium-high heat until drop of batter sizzles. Working in batches, scoop mixture by scant $1/2$ cupfuls into hot oil; flatten slightly with bottom of measuring cup. Cook 3 minutes per side or until golden brown. Drain on paper towels. Serve with applesauce.

If you don't have a spiralizer, shred potatoes on the large holes of a box grater.

2 small *or* 1 large sweet potato (about 1 pound), peeled

1 russet potato (about 12 ounces)

1 shallot, minced

3 eggs

$1/3$ cup all-purpose flour

$1/2$ teaspoon salt

$1/4$ teaspoon baking powder

$1/8$ teaspoon ground nutmeg

1 cup vegetable oil for frying

Applesauce for serving

OVERNIGHT CHIA OAT PUDDING

MAKES 4 SERVINGS (2 CUPS)

1. Combine oats, chia seeds, 2 tablespoons sugar, cinnamon and salt in medium bowl or food storage container. Add oat milk; stir until well blended. Cover and refrigerate overnight.

2. Combine strawberries and remaining 1 tablespoon sugar in another medium bowl or food storage container. Cover and refrigerate overnight.

3. Stir oat mixture. Fold blueberries into strawberries, if desired. For each serving, scoop $1/2$ cup oat mixture into bowl. Top with berries, 1 tablespoon pecans and banana, if desired.

- 1 cup old-fashioned oats
- $1/4$ cup chia seeds
- 3 tablespoons palm sugar or brown sugar, divided
- $1/2$ teaspoon ground cinnamon
- $1/2$ teaspoon salt
- $1^3/_4$ cups oat milk
- 1 package (1 pound) fresh strawberries, stemmed and diced
- 1 cup fresh blueberries (optional)
- 4 tablespoons chopped pecans or sliced almonds
- 4 bananas, sliced (optional)

BREAKFAST QUINOA
MAKES 2 SERVINGS

1. Place quinoa in fine-mesh strainer; rinse well under cold running water. Transfer to small saucepan.

2. Stir in 1 cup water, brown sugar, maple syrup, cinnamon and salt; bring to a boil over high heat. Reduce heat to low; cover and simmer 10 to 15 minutes or until quinoa is tender and water is absorbed. Add raisins, if desired, during last 5 minutes of cooking.

3. Scoop quinoa into bowls; top with raspberries and bananas. Serve with oat milk, if desired.

NOTE: This recipe scales up very easily to make additional servings. Simply double or triple the ingredients to make as much as you want. It also reheats really well in the microwave, so you can make a large batch and refrigerate individual portions for quick breakfasts.

- $\frac{1}{2}$ cup uncooked quinoa
- 1 cup water
- 1 tablespoon packed brown sugar or palm sugar
- 2 teaspoons maple syrup
- $\frac{1}{2}$ teaspoon ground cinnamon
- $\frac{1}{2}$ teaspoon salt
- $\frac{1}{4}$ cup golden raisins (optional)

  Fresh raspberries and banana slices

  Oat milk (optional)

SCRAMBLED TOFU AND POTATOES

MAKES 4 SERVINGS

1. For potatoes, preheat oven to 450°F. Pour ¼ cup oil into 12-inch cast-iron skillet; place skillet in oven 10 minutes to heat.

2. Bring large saucepan of water to a boil. Add potatoes; cook 5 to 7 minutes or until tender. Drain and return to saucepan; stir in sliced onion, rosemary and salt. Spread mixture in preheated skillet. Bake 25 to 30 minutes or until potatoes are browned, stirring every 10 minutes.

3. For tofu, combine nutritional yeast and turmeric in small bowl. Stir in water and soy sauce until smooth. Cut tofu into large cubes. Gently squeeze out water; loosely crumble tofu into medium bowl.

4. Heat 2 teaspoons oil in large nonstick skillet over medium-high heat. Add bell pepper and red onion; cook and stir 2 minutes or until soft but not browned. Add tofu; drizzle with 3 tablespoons nutritional yeast sauce. Cook and stir about 5 minutes or until liquid is evaporated and tofu is heated through. Stir in additional sauce for stronger flavor, if desired.

5. Divide potatoes among four serving plates; top with tofu mixture.

POTATOES

- ¼ cup olive oil
- 4 red potatoes, cubed
- ½ yellow onion, sliced
- 1 tablespoon chopped fresh rosemary
- 1 teaspoon salt

SCRAMBLED TOFU

- ¼ cup nutritional yeast
- ½ teaspoon ground turmeric
- 2 tablespoons water
- 2 tablespoons soy sauce
- 1 package (14 to 16 ounces) firm tofu
- 2 teaspoons olive oil
- ½ cup chopped green bell pepper
- ½ cup chopped red onion

BREAKFAST RICE PUDDING
MAKES 4 SERVINGS

1. Bring 1$\frac{1}{2}$ cups oat milk to a simmer in medium saucepan over medium-high heat. Stir in rice, oats, sugar, cinnamon and salt until well blended. Reduce heat to low; cover and simmer 10 minutes.

2. Stir in remaining $\frac{1}{2}$ cup oat milk and raisins, if desired; cover and simmer 10 minutes. Remove from heat; stir in vanilla and almond extract. Scoop into bowls; top with berries.

NOTE: Rice pudding thickens as it cools. For a thinner consistency, stir in additional oat milk.

2 cups oat milk, divided

$\frac{1}{2}$ cup quick-cooking brown rice*

$\frac{1}{4}$ cup old-fashioned oats

$\frac{1}{3}$ cup palm sugar or packed brown sugar

$\frac{1}{2}$ teaspoon ground cinnamon

$\frac{1}{8}$ teaspoon salt

$\frac{1}{4}$ cup golden raisins (optional)

$\frac{1}{2}$ teaspoon vanilla

$\frac{1}{8}$ teaspoon almond extract

Fresh or thawed frozen mixed berries

Look for rice that cooks in 20 to 25 minutes. For rice with a longer cooking time, increase the cooking time according to package directions in step 1.

PUMPKIN GRANOLA
MAKES ABOUT 6 CUPS

1. Preheat oven to 325°F. Line large rimmed baking sheet with parchment paper.

2. Combine oats, almonds and pepitas in large bowl. Combine pumpkin, maple syrup, oil, cinnamon, vanilla, salt, ginger, nutmeg and cloves in medium bowl; stir until well blended. Pour over oat mixture; stir until well blended and all ingredients are completely coated. Spread evenly on prepared baking sheet.

3. Bake 50 to 60 minutes or until granola is golden brown and no longer moist, stirring every 20 minutes. (Granola will become more crisp as it cools.) Stir in cranberries; cool completely.

VARIATIONS: For Pumpkin Chocolate Granola, follow recipe above but reduce amount of maple syrup to $1/3$ cup. Stir in $3/4$ cup semisweet chocolate chips after baking. You can substitute pecans or walnuts for the almonds, and/or add $3/4$ cup flaked coconut to the mixture before baking.

3 cups old-fashioned oats

$3/4$ cup coarsely chopped almonds

$3/4$ cup pepitas (raw pumpkin seeds)

$1/2$ cup canned pumpkin

$1/2$ cup maple syrup

$1/3$ cup coconut oil, melted

1 teaspoon ground cinnamon

1 teaspoon vanilla

$1/2$ teaspoon salt

$1/4$ teaspoon ground ginger

$1/4$ teaspoon ground nutmeg

Pinch of ground cloves

$3/4$ cup dried cranberries

BLUEBERRY BANANA OATMEAL SMOOTHIE

MAKES 1 TO 2 SERVINGS

1. Combine oat milk, banana and blueberries in blender; blend until smooth. Add yogurt and oats; blend until smooth.

2. Pour into glass; serve immediately.

1 cup oat milk

1 banana

1/2 cup frozen blueberries

1 container (5 ounces) plain or vanilla nondairy or regular yogurt (about 1/2 cup)

1/4 cup old-fashioned oats

BREAKFAST POM SMOOTHIE

MAKES 1 TO 2 SERVINGS

1. Combine juice, banana and berries in blender; blend until smooth. Add $1/3$ cup soymilk; blend until smooth. Add additional soymilk for thinner consistency, if desired; blend until smooth.

2. Pour into glass; serve immediately.

$3/4$ **cup pomegranate juice**

1 **banana**

$1/2$ **cup frozen mixed berries**

$1/3$ **to** $1/2$ **cup soymilk**

BANANA OATMEAL BREAKFAST COOKIES

MAKES ABOUT 3 DOZEN COOKIES

1. Stir 6 tablespoons boiling water into flaxseed in small bowl. Cool completely; refrigerate until ready to use. Place raisins in small bowl. Pour remaining $1/3$ cup boiling water over raisins; set aside.

2. Preheat oven to 375°F. Line cookie sheets with parchment paper. Combine oats, flour, cinnamon, baking soda, salt, nutmeg and cardamom in medium bowl.

3. Beat sugar and butter in large bowl with electric mixer at medium speed until creamy. Add bananas and flaxseed mixture; beat until well blended. Gradually add oat mixture at low speed, beating until stiff dough forms. Drain raisins. Stir raisins and pecans into dough.

4. Drop dough by heaping tablespoonfuls 2 inches apart onto prepared cookie sheets.

5. Bake 10 to 12 minutes or until edges are set and lightly browned. Cool on cookie sheets 1 minute. Remove to wire racks; cool completely.

$1/3$ **cup plus 6 tablespoons boiling water, divided**

2 **tablespoons ground flaxseed**

1 **cup raisins**

2 **cups old-fashioned oats**

2 **cups all-purpose flour**

1 **tablespoon ground cinnamon**

1 **teaspoon baking soda**

1 **teaspoon salt**

$1/2$ **teaspoon ground nutmeg**

$1/4$ **teaspoon ground cardamom**

$1^{1}/_{2}$ **cups palm sugar or packed brown sugar**

$3/4$ **cup ($1^{1}/_{2}$ sticks) vegan plant butter or regular butter, softened**

3 **bananas, mashed**

$1/2$ **cup chopped pecans**

ZUCCHINI DATE BREAD

MAKES 1 LOAF (12 TO 16 SERVINGS)

1. Preheat oven to 350°F. Spray 8×4-inch loaf pan with nonstick cooking spray.

2. Combine dates and water in small saucepan; bring to a boil over medium-high heat. Remove from heat; let stand 15 minutes.

3. Combine all-purpose flour, whole wheat flour, sugar, baking powder, baking soda, salt, cinnamon and cloves in large bowl. Beat eggs in medium bowl; stir in date mixture and zucchini. Stir egg mixture into flour mixture just until moistened. Pour into prepared pan.

4. Bake 30 to 35 minutes or until toothpick inserted into center comes out clean. Cool in pan 5 minutes. Remove to wire rack; cool completely.

NOTE: To make this recipe vegan, substitute flaxseed for the eggs. Combine 6 tablespoons boiling water and 2 tablespoons ground flaxseed in a small bowl and let it cool completely. You can make the mixture ahead and store it in the refrigerator until you're ready to use it.

1 cup chopped pitted dates

1 cup water

1 cup all-purpose flour

1 cup whole wheat flour

2 tablespoons sugar

1 teaspoon baking powder

1/2 teaspoon baking soda

1/2 teaspoon salt

1/2 teaspoon ground cinnamon

1/4 teaspoon ground cloves

2 eggs

1 cup shredded zucchini,* pressed dry with paper towels

Grate zucchini on the large holes of a box grater.

SALADS

TOMATO, CUCUMBER AND WHITE BEAN SALAD

MAKES 4 SERVINGS

1. Combine beans, tomatoes, cucumber, onion and cilantro in large bowl.

2. Whisk oil, lime juice, salt and pepper in small bowl. Pour over salad; mix gently.

TIP: This simple dish is a versatile and easy addition to your salad repertoire. Fold in diced avocado (or crumbled feta or goat cheese if you're doing dairy) to make it more substantial. To use it as a topping for crostini or sandwich filling, slightly mash the beans before adding the remaining ingredients. Add minced canned chipotle pepper to add zesty heat, or swap basil for the cilantro and red or white wine vinegar for the lime juice to change the flavor profile.

1 cup canned Great Northern beans or chickpeas, rinsed and drained

1 cup halved grape tomatoes

1 cup diced cucumber ($1/2$-inch pieces)

2 tablespoons finely diced red onion

1 tablespoon finely chopped fresh cilantro

1 tablespoon olive oil

1 tablespoon lime juice

$1/4$ teaspoon salt

$1/8$ teaspoon black pepper

GREEK SALAD WITH TOFU "FETA"

MAKES 4 TO 6 SERVINGS

1. For "feta," cut tofu crosswise into two pieces, each about 1 inch thick. Place on cutting board lined with paper towels; top with layer of paper towels. Place weighted baking dish on top of tofu. Let stand 30 minutes to drain. Pat tofu dry and crumble into large bowl.

2. Combine oil, lemon juice, salt, Greek seasoning and black pepper in small jar with lid; shake until well blended. Reserve 1/4 cup mixture for salad dressing. Add onion powder and garlic powder to remaining mixture; pour over tofu and toss gently. Cover and refrigerate 2 hours or overnight.

3. For salad, combine tomatoes, cucumbers, bell pepper and onion in serving bowl. Add tofu and reserved dressing. Toss gently to mix.

TOFU "FETA"

- 1 package (14 to 16 ounces) firm or extra firm tofu
- 1/2 cup olive oil
- 1/4 cup lemon juice
- 2 teaspoons salt
- 2 teaspoons Greek or Italian seasoning
- 1/2 teaspoon black pepper
- 1 teaspoon onion powder
- 1/2 teaspoon garlic powder

SALAD

- 1 pint grape tomatoes, halved
- 2 seedless cucumbers, quartered lengthwise and sliced
- 1 yellow bell pepper, thinly sliced
- 1 small red onion, thinly sliced

PEPITA LIME CABBAGE SLAW
MAKES 6 TO 8 SERVINGS (8 CUPS)

1. Place onion in large bowl. Add vinegar, sugar and 1 teaspoon salt; mix well. Let stand at least 20 minutes. Combine cumin, onion powder, coriander and celery seed in small bowl.

2. Meanwhile, heat 2 teaspoons oil in small skillet over medium heat. Add pepitas; cook and stir 5 minutes or until pepitas begin to brown and pop. Season with pepper and remaining $1/2$ teaspoon salt. Spread on plate; cool completely.

3. Add green cabbage, red cabbage and cilantro to onion in large bowl. Drizzle with lime juice and remaining 1 tablespoon oil; sprinkle with seasoning mix. Mix thoroughly with hands, squeezing to blend everything evenly. Sprinkle with pepitas; toss gently to blend.

NOTE: This recipe can be made a day ahead. Store it in a large covered bowl or container, and adjust salt, pepper and lime juice before serving. To keep the pepitas crisp, stir them in just before serving.

- $1/2$ red onion, thinly sliced
- 3 tablespoons cider vinegar
- 1 teaspoon sugar
- $1 1/2$ teaspoons salt, divided
- $1/2$ teaspoon ground cumin
- $1/4$ teaspoon onion powder
- $1/8$ teaspoon ground coriander
- $1/8$ teaspoon celery seed
- 1 tablespoon plus 2 teaspoons olive oil, divided
- $1/2$ cup pepitas (raw pumpkin seeds)
- $1/8$ teaspoon black pepper
- 4 cups thinly sliced green cabbage (about $1/8$ head)
- 4 cups thinly sliced red cabbage (about $1/2$ small head)
- 3 tablespoons chopped fresh cilantro
- 2 tablespoons lime juice

FRENCH LENTIL SALAD

MAKES 4 SERVINGS

1. Combine water and lentils in large saucepan; bring to a boil over high heat. Reduce heat to low; simmer about 20 minutes or until lentils are tender but not mushy, stirring occasionally. Drain lentils and place in large bowl.

2. Add green onions, vinegar, parsley, oil, salt, thyme and pepper to lentils; mix well. Cover and refrigerate 1 hour or until cool.

3. Top with walnuts just before serving.

8 cups water

1½ cups dried lentils, rinsed and sorted

4 green onions, finely chopped

3 tablespoons balsamic vinegar

2 tablespoons chopped fresh parsley

1 tablespoon olive oil

1 teaspoon salt

½ teaspoon dried thyme

¼ teaspoon black pepper

¼ cup chopped walnuts, toasted*

To toast walnuts, spread in small skillet. Cook over medium heat 2 to 4 minutes until lightly browned and fragrant, stirring frequently.

SZECHUAN-STYLE TOFU SALAD

MAKES 4 SERVINGS

1. Combine soy sauce, canola oil, sesame oil, ginger and hot pepper sauce in small bowl.

2. Drain tofu and place between two paper towels; press lightly to drain excess water from tofu. Cut tofu into 1-inch cubes. Place in shallow dish. Drizzle 2 tablespoons soy sauce mixture over tofu cubes.

3. Combine spinach, cabbage, sugar snap peas, carrots, bean sprouts and remaining soy sauce mixture in large bowl; toss to coat.

4. Divide salad among flour plates. Top each serving evenly with tofu mixture, peanuts and cilantro.

1/4 cup soy sauce

1 tablespoon canola or peanut oil

1 tablespoon toasted sesame oil

1 teaspoon minced fresh ginger

1/2 teaspoon hot pepper sauce

1 package (14 to 16 ounces) extra firm tofu

4 cups baby spinach

4 cups sliced napa or green cabbage

2 cups diagonally halved fresh sugar snap peas or snow peas

1 cup julienned carrots

1 cup fresh bean sprouts

1/4 cup dry-roasted peanuts or toasted slivered almonds

Chopped fresh cilantro or green onions

MARINATED TOMATO SALAD

MAKES 8 SERVINGS

1. Combine vinegar and salt in large bowl; stir until salt is completely dissolved. Add shallots, chives, lemon juice and pepper; mix well. Slowly whisk in oil until well blended.

2. Add tomatoes to marinade; toss well. Cover; let stand at room temperature 30 minutes or up to 2 hours before serving.

3. To serve, remove tomatoes from marinade using slotted spoon; place on serving plates. Garnish with sprouts.

1½ **cups white wine vinegar**

½ **teaspoon salt**

¼ **cup finely chopped shallots**

2 **tablespoons finely chopped fresh chives**

2 **tablespoons fresh lemon juice**

¼ **teaspoon white pepper**

2 **tablespoons olive oil**

6 **plum tomatoes, quartered**

2 **large yellow tomatoes,* cut into ½-inch-thick slices**

16 **red cherry tomatoes, halved**

16 **small yellow pear tomatoes,* halved (optional)**

Sunflower sprouts (optional)

*Substitute an additional 10 plum tomatoes, quartered, for yellow tomatoes and yellow pear tomatoes, if desired.

PEAR ARUGULA SALAD

MAKES 4 SERVINGS

1. For pecans, preheat oven to 350°F. Line small baking sheet with foil; spray foil with nonstick cooking spray. Combine pecans, brown sugar, butter, honey, 1/4 teaspoon salt and cinnamon in medium skillet. Cook and stir 2 to 3 minutes or until sugar and butter are melted and nuts are glazed. Spread on foil. Bake 5 to 7 minutes or until nuts are fragrant and a shade darker. Remove foil from baking sheet; cool nuts completely on foil.

2. For dressing, whisk oil, vinegar, molasses, mustard, 1/2 teaspoon salt, thyme and pepper in small bowl until smooth and well blended.

3. Divide arugula among four bowls. Top with pears, nuts and cheese, if desired; drizzle each serving with 2 tablespoons dressing.

NOTE: For a heartier salad, serve with a scoop of cooked red quinoa and top with dried cherries or cranberries.

CARAMELIZED PECANS

- 1/2 cup pecan halves
- 3 tablespoons packed brown sugar
- 1 tablespoon butter or vegan plant butter
- 1 tablespoon honey
- 1/4 teaspoon salt
- 1/8 teaspoon ground cinnamon

DRESSING

- 1/4 cup olive oil
- 3 tablespoons balsamic vinegar
- 1 teaspoon pomegranate molasses or honey
- 1 teaspoon Dijon mustard
- 1/2 teaspoon salt
- 1/4 teaspoon dried thyme
- 1/8 teaspoon black pepper

SALAD

- 2 cups arugula
- 2 red pears, thinly sliced
- 1/2 cup crumbled gorgonzola or blue cheese (optional)

COUSCOUS AND BLACK BEAN SALAD

MAKES 4 SERVINGS

1. Bring water, 1 tablespoon oil and $1/4$ teaspoon salt to a boil in small saucepan. Stir in couscous. Cover and remove from heat; let stand 5 minutes. Fluff with fork. Spread couscous on large baking sheet to cool.

2. Combine couscous and black beans in large bowl. Cut tomatoes in half lengthwise, reserving 1 tablespoon of accumulated tomato juice. Add tomatoes to couscous. Stir in chives, cilantro and jalapeño pepper, if desired; mix gently.

3. Whisk remaining 1 tablespoon oil, vinegar, reserved tomato juice, remaining $1/4$ teaspoon salt and black pepper in small bowl until well blended. Pour over salad; toss lightly to coat.

1 cup water

2 tablespoons olive oil, divided

$1/2$ teaspoon salt, divided

$3/4$ cup uncooked whole wheat couscous

1 can (about 15 ounces) black beans, rinsed and drained

1 cup cherry tomatoes

2 tablespoons minced fresh chives or green onion (green parts only)

1 tablespoon minced fresh cilantro

1 jalapeño pepper, seeded and minced (optional)

2 teaspoons white wine vinegar

$1/8$ teaspoon black pepper

ROASTED POTATO SALAD WITH CAPERS AND WALNUTS

MAKES 6 TO 8 SERVINGS

1. Preheat oven to 400°F.

2. Slash bottoms of brussels sprouts; place in shallow roasting pan. Add potatoes; sprinkle with salt, black pepper and rosemary. Drizzle with 3 tablespoons oil; toss to coat.

3. Roast 20 minutes. Stir in bell pepper; roast 15 minutes or until vegetables are tender. Transfer to large bowl; stir in walnuts and capers.

4. Whisk remaining 2 tablespoons oil and vinegar in small bowl until blended. Pour over salad; toss to coat. Serve at room temperature.

1 pound small brussels sprouts, trimmed

1 pound small Yukon Gold potatoes, halved

$\frac{1}{2}$ teaspoon salt

$\frac{1}{4}$ teaspoon black pepper

$\frac{1}{4}$ teaspoon dried rosemary

5 tablespoons olive oil, divided

1 red bell pepper, cut into bite-size pieces

$\frac{1}{4}$ cup coarsely chopped walnuts

2 tablespoons capers, drained

$1\frac{1}{2}$ tablespoons white wine vinegar

EDAMAME PEANUT SALAD

MAKES 6 TO 8 SERVINGS (8 CUPS)

1. Combine green cabbage, red cabbage, bell pepper, edamame, green onions and carrot in large bowl.

2. Whisk lime juice, vinegar, oil, salt, sugar and ginger in small bowl until salt and sugar are dissolved. Pour dressing over salad; mix well. Stir in peanuts just before serving.

NOTE: This salad can be made a day ahead of time, but will even be good for several days. Store it in a covered bowl or container and adjust the salt, lime juice and vinegar before serving. For crunchy peanuts, stir them in just before serving. They will also be fine if you stir them in early and let them sit. Their texture will be more crisp-tender than crisp, similar to the edamame.

4 cups thinly sliced green cabbage (about $1/8$ head)

3 cups thinly sliced red cabbage (about $1/2$ small head)

1 red bell pepper, thinly sliced

1 cup thawed frozen shelled edamame

3 green onions, thinly sliced

1 carrot, shredded or julienned

Juice of 1 lime

2 tablespoons unseasoned rice vinegar

1 tablespoon toasted sesame oil

2 teaspoons salt

1 teaspoon sugar

1 teaspoon minced fresh ginger

1 cup dry roasted peanuts

BLACK BEAN GAZPACHO SALAD

MAKES 4 TO 6 SERVINGS

1. Combine beans, tomatoes, corn, cucumber, onion and cilantro in large bowl.

2. Whisk tomato juice, lime juice, oil, chili powder and salt in small bowl. Pour over salad; toss to blend. Season with pepper.

1 can (about 15 ounces) black beans, rinsed and drained

2 cups diced tomatoes

1$\frac{1}{3}$ cups fresh or thawed frozen corn

1 cup diced cucumber

$\frac{1}{4}$ cup diced red onion

2 tablespoons finely chopped fresh cilantro

$\frac{1}{3}$ cup tomato juice

3 tablespoons lime juice

2 tablespoons olive oil

1 teaspoon chili powder

$\frac{1}{2}$ teaspoon salt

Black pepper

KALE SALAD WITH CHERRIES AND AVOCADOS

MAKES 6 TO 8 SERVINGS

1. Heat 1 teaspoon oil in small saucepan over medium-high heat. Add quinoa; cook and stir 3 to 5 minutes or until quinoa is golden brown and popped. Season with 1/4 teaspoon salt. Spread on plate; cool completely.

2. Combine balsamic vinegar, red wine vinegar, maple syrup, mustard, oregano, pepper and remaining 1/2 teaspoon salt in medium bowl. Whisk in remaining 1/4 cup oil until well blended.

3. Place kale in large bowl. Pour dressing over kale; massage dressing into leaves until well blended and kale is slightly softened. Add popped quinoa; stir until well blended. Add cherries, avocados and almonds; toss until blended.

NOTE: Kale is very hearty and will keep for several days in the refrigerator without becoming mushy, making this a great salad to make ahead or pack into individual containers to take for lunches.

1/4 cup plus 1 teaspoon olive oil, divided

3 tablespoons uncooked quinoa

3/4 teaspoon salt, divided

3 tablespoons balsamic vinegar

1 tablespoon red wine vinegar

1 tablespoon maple syrup

2 teaspoons Dijon mustard

1/4 teaspoon dried oregano

1/8 teaspoon black pepper

1 large bunch kale (about 1 pound)

1 package (5 ounces) dried cherries

2 avocados, diced

1/2 cup smoked almonds, chopped

ROASTED VEGETABLE SPINACH SALAD

MAKES 4 SERVINGS

1. Preheat oven to 375°F. Spray large rimmed baking sheet with nonstick cooking spray.

2. Combine mushrooms, carrots, bell peppers, tomatoes, onion, olives, oil, 2 teaspoons lemon juice, oregano, salt and black pepper in large bowl; toss to coat. Spread vegetables in single layer on prepared baking sheet.

3. Roast 20 minutes or until carrots are tender and mushrooms are browned, stirring once. Stir in remaining 2 teaspoons lemon juice and sugar, if desired. Toss with spinach; serve warm.

2 cups sliced mushrooms

2 cups sliced carrots

2 cups chopped yellow or green bell peppers (1-inch pieces)

2 cups cherry or grape tomatoes, halved

1 cup chopped or sliced onion

1/4 cup chopped pitted kalamata olives

2 tablespoons olive oil

4 teaspoons lemon juice, divided

1 1/2 teaspoons dried oregano

1 teaspoon salt

1/2 teaspoon black pepper

1 teaspoon sugar (optional)

3 cups packed baby spinach

ARTICHOKE SALAD ON TOMATOES

MAKES 4 SERVINGS

1. Combine artichokes, mushrooms, parsley and green onions in medium bowl. Add dressing, basil, and garlic; toss until well blended. Season with salt and pepper. Stir in blue cheese, if desired.

2. Arrange 2 tomato slices on each salad plate; top with artichoke mixture.

TIP: You can purchase bottled Italian salad dressing for this recipe or you can easily make it yourself. Combine 3 tablespoons white or red wine vinegar, 1 tablespoon Dijon mustard, 1 minced garlic clove, 1 teaspoon honey, $\frac{1}{2}$ teaspoon salt, $\frac{1}{2}$ teaspoon onion powder, $\frac{1}{4}$ teaspoon dried basil, $\frac{1}{4}$ teaspoon dried oregano, and a pinch of red pepper flakes or black pepper in a medium bowl. Whisk in $\frac{1}{3}$ cup olive oil in a thin steady stream until well blended. Or combine all ingredients in a jar with a tight-fitting lid and shake until the dressing is well blended. Store dressing in a jar in the refrigerator.

1 can (about 14 ounces) artichoke hearts, drained and coarsely chopped

1 package (8 ounces) sliced white or cremini mushrooms

$\frac{1}{4}$ cup minced fresh parsley

2 green onions, chopped

$\frac{1}{4}$ cup Italian salad dressing (see Tip)

1 tablespoon chopped fresh basil leaves

1 clove garlic, minced

Salt and black pepper

3 tablespoons crumbled blue cheese (optional)

1 medium tomato, cut into 8 slices

FATTOUSH SALAD

MAKES 4 TO 6 SERVINGS

1. Preheat oven to 400°F. Cut pita breads into 1-inch cubes. Toss with 3 tablespoons oil and ½ teaspoon salt in large bowl. Spread on large rimmed baking sheet. Bake 10 minutes or until pita cubes are browned and crisp. Cool completely on baking sheet.

2. Combine lettuce, cucumber, tomatoes, green onions, radishes, parsley and mint in large bowl. Add pita cubes.

3. For dressing, combine remaining ⅓ cup oil, molasses, garlic, vinegar, lemon juice and sumac, if desired, in small bowl. Season with remaining ½ teaspoon salt and pepper; whisk until well blended. Taste and adjust seasonings. Pour over salad; toss until well blended.

2 pita breads

⅓ cup plus 3 tablespoons olive oil, divided

1 teaspoon salt, divided

2 cups chopped romaine or green leaf lettuce

1 seedless cucumber, quartered lengthwise and sliced

2 tomatoes, diced

4 green onions, thinly sliced

3 radishes, thinly sliced

¼ cup finely chopped fresh parsley

1 tablespoon finely chopped fresh mint

2 tablespoons pomegranate molasses

2 cloves garlic, minced

2 tablespoons red wine vinegar

1 tablespoon lemon juice

½ teaspoon ground sumac (optional)

Black pepper

SOUPS & STEWS

CLASSIC VEGETABLE SOUP

MAKES 4 TO 6 SERVINGS

1. Heat oil in large saucepan over medium-high heat. Add onion, carrot and garlic; cook and stir 5 minutes or until onion is tender. Add tomato paste, basil, oregano and salt; cook and stir 1 minute.

2. Add broth; bring to a boil. Reduce heat to medium-low. Add cabbage, green beans and zucchini; simmer 10 to 15 minutes or until vegetables are tender.

- 1 tablespoon vegetable or olive oil
- 1 onion, chopped
- $2/3$ cup carrot slices
- 2 cloves garlic, minced
- 1 tablespoon tomato paste
- $1/2$ teaspoon dried basil
- $1/2$ teaspoon dried oregano
- $1/4$ teaspoon salt
- 4 cups (32 ounces) vegetable broth
- 2 cups chopped green cabbage
- $1/2$ cup cut green beans (1-inch pieces)
- $1/2$ cup diced zucchini

CURRY RED LENTIL AND CHICKPEA STEW
MAKES 4 TO 6 SERVINGS

1. Heat oil in large saucepan over medium-high heat. Add onion; cook and stir 5 minutes or until softened. Add garlic, ginger, curry powder, turmeric, salt and red pepper; cook and stir 1 minute. Add broth; bring to a boil. Stir in lentils; cook 15 minutes.

2. Stir in chickpeas and coconut milk; cook 5 to 10 minutes or until lentils are tender, chickpeas are hot and stew is slightly thickened. Stir in spinach; cook and stir just until spinach is wilted. Ladle into bowls; sprinkle with cilantro, if desired.

1 tablespoon olive oil

1 onion, chopped

3 cloves garlic, minced

2 tablespoons minced fresh ginger

1 tablespoon curry powder

2 teaspoons ground turmeric

$1\frac{1}{2}$ teaspoons salt

$\frac{1}{8}$ teaspoon ground red pepper

4 cups (32 ounces) vegetable broth

$1\frac{1}{4}$ cups uncooked red lentils (8 ounces)

1 can (about 15 ounces) chickpeas, rinsed and drained

1 can (14 ounces) unsweetened coconut milk

1 package (5 ounces) baby spinach

Chopped fresh cilantro and/or unsweetened dried coconut slices (optional)

FASOLADA (GREEK WHITE BEAN SOUP)

MAKES 4 TO 6 SERVINGS

1. Heat 2 tablespoons oil in large saucepan over medium-high heat. Add onion, celery and carrots; cook and stir 8 to 10 minutes or until vegetables are softened. Stir in garlic; cook and stir 30 seconds. Stir in tomato paste, salt, oregano, cumin, pepper and bay leaf; cook and stir 30 seconds.

2. Stir in broth; bring to a boil. Stir in beans; return to a boil. Reduce heat to medium-low; simmer 30 minutes. Stir in remaining 2 tablespoons oil and lemon juice. Ladle into bowls; sprinkle with parsley.

- 4 tablespoons olive oil, divided
- 1 large onion, chopped
- 3 stalks celery, diced
- 3 carrots, diced
- 4 cloves garlic, minced
- 1/4 cup tomato paste
- 1 teaspoon salt
- 1 teaspoon dried oregano
- 1/2 teaspoon ground cumin
- 1/4 teaspoon black pepper
- 1 bay leaf
- 4 cups (32 ounces) vegetable broth
- 3 cans (about 15 ounces each) cannellini beans, rinsed and drained
- 2 tablespoons lemon juice
- 1/4 cup minced fresh parsley

CORN, ZUCCHINI AND BLACK BEAN STEW

MAKES 4 SERVINGS

1. Heat oil in large saucepan over medium heat. Add onion; cook and stir 5 minutes or until softened. Add garlic, chili powder and cumin; cook and stir 1 minute.

2. Stir in tomatoes, salsa, zucchini, beans and corn; bring to a boil over high heat. Reduce heat to low; cover and simmer 20 minutes or until vegetables are tender. Season to taste with salt and black pepper. Ladle into bowls; top with desired toppings.

1 tablespoon canola or vegetable oil

1 onion, chopped

4 cloves garlic, minced

2 teaspoons chili powder

1 teaspoon ground cumin

1 can (about 14 ounces) fire-roasted diced tomatoes

3/4 cup salsa

2 medium zucchini or yellow squash (or 1 of each), cut into 1/2-inch chunks

1 can (about 15 ounces) black beans, rinsed and drained

1 cup frozen corn

Salt and black pepper

Optional toppings: chopped fresh cilantro, chopped green onion and/or minced jalapeno peppers

LIMA BEAN AND ESCAROLE SOUP

MAKES 6 SERVINGS

1. Place lima beans in large bowl; add water to cover by at least 2 inches. Soak 6 to 8 hours or overnight.

2. Drain beans; place in large saucepan or Dutch oven. Add 3 cups water; bring to a boil over high heat. Reduce heat to low. Cover and simmer about 1 hour or until soft. Drain and return to saucepan.

3. Heat oil in small skillet over medium heat. Add celery, onion and garlic; cook and stir 5 minutes or until onion is tender.

4. Add celery mixture and tomatoes to beans. Stir in parsley, rosemary, salt and pepper. Cover and simmer over low heat 15 minutes. Add escarole; simmer 5 minutes. Taste and adjust seasonings.

TIP: The easiest way to chop the tomatoes for this recipe doesn't use a knife at all. Working with one tomato at a time, squeeze them through your fingers into the saucepan, then add the juice.

$1\frac{1}{2}$ cups dried baby lima beans, rinsed and sorted

3 cups water

1 teaspoon olive oil

$\frac{1}{2}$ cup chopped celery

$\frac{1}{2}$ cup chopped onion

2 cloves garlic, minced

1 can (28 ounces) whole tomatoes, chopped and juice reserved

$\frac{1}{2}$ cup chopped fresh parsley

2 tablespoons chopped fresh rosemary

1 teaspoon salt

$\frac{1}{4}$ teaspoon black pepper

3 cups shredded fresh escarole

ITALIAN BEAN AND VEGETABLE SOUP

MAKES 4 SERVINGS

1. Heat 1 tablespoon oil in large saucepan or Dutch oven over medium-high heat. Add bell pepper; cook and stir 4 minutes or until softened. Add garlic; cook and stir 30 seconds. Add water, tomatoes, zucchini and red pepper flakes; bring to a boil. Reduce heat to low; cover and simmer 20 minutes.

2. Add beans, basil, remaining 1 tablespoon oil, vinegar and salt; simmer 5 minutes. Remove from heat; let stand, covered, 10 minutes before serving.

2 tablespoons olive oil, divided

1 medium orange or red bell pepper, chopped

1 clove garlic, minced

2 cups water

1 can (about 14 ounces) fire-roasted diced tomatoes

1 medium zucchini, thinly sliced lengthwise

$1/8$ teaspoon red pepper flakes

1 can (about 15 ounces) navy beans, rinsed and drained

3 tablespoons chopped fresh basil

1 tablespoon balsamic vinegar

$3/4$ teaspoon salt

HOT AND SOUR SOUP WITH TOFU

MAKES 4 SERVINGS

1. Heat oil in large saucepan over medium heat. Add mushrooms and garlic; cook and stir 3 minutes. Add broth, 1 cup water, soy sauce, vinegar and red pepper flakes; bring to a boil. Reduce heat to medium; simmer 5 minutes.

2. Whisk remaining 2 tablespoons water into cornstarch in small bowl until smooth. Stir into soup; cook 2 minutes or until thickened.

3. Stir in bok choy; cook 2 to 3 minutes or until wilted. Stir in tofu; cook until heated through. Ladle soup into bowls; sprinkle with green onion.

1 tablespoon toasted sesame oil

4 ounces fresh shiitake mushrooms, stems finely chopped, caps thinly sliced

2 cloves garlic, minced

2 cups mushroom broth or vegetable broth

1 cup plus 2 tablespoons water, divided

2 tablespoons soy sauce

1 1/2 tablespoons rice vinegar or white wine vinegar

1/4 teaspoon red pepper flakes

1 1/2 tablespoons cornstarch

2 cups coarsely chopped bok choy leaves or napa cabbage

10 ounces silken extra firm tofu, drained and cut into 1/2-inch cubes

1 green onion, thinly sliced

MIDDLE EASTERN LENTIL SOUP

MAKES 4 SERVINGS

1. Heat oil in large saucepan over medium-high heat. Add onion and bell pepper; cook and stir 5 minutes or until tender. Add fennel seeds, cumin and ground red pepper; cook and stir 1 minute.

2. Add water, lentils and salt; bring to a boil. Reduce heat to low; cover and simmer 25 to 30 minutes or until lentils are tender. Stir in lemon juice.

3. Ladle soup into bowls and top with yogurt, if desired; sprinkle with parsley.

NOTE: Packages of dried lentils can contain dirt and tiny stones, so it is a good idea to thoroughly rinse them. Then sort through the lentils and pick out any unusual looking pieces.

2 tablespoons olive oil

1 onion, chopped

1 red bell pepper, chopped

1 teaspoon whole fennel seeds

$1/2$ teaspoon ground cumin

$1/4$ teaspoon ground red pepper

4 cups water

1 cup dried lentils, rinsed and sorted (see Note)

1 teaspoon salt

1 tablespoon lemon juice

Plain yogurt or sour cream (optional)

Chopped fresh parsley

ZESTY VEGETABLE CHILI

MAKES 4 SERVINGS

1. Heat oil in large saucepan over medium heat. Add bell pepper; cook and stir 4 minutes. Add zucchini and garlic; cook and stir 3 minutes.

2. Stir in tomatoes, salsa, chili powder, oregano, salt and pepper; bring to a boil over high heat. Reduce heat to low; simmer 15 minutes or until vegetables are tender.

3. Stir in beans; simmer 2 minutes or until heated through. Stir in tofu; remove from heat. Ladle into bowls; garnish with cilantro.

1 tablespoon canola or vegetable oil

1 red bell pepper, chopped

2 medium zucchini or yellow squash (or 1 of each), cut into $1/2$-inch chunks

4 cloves garlic, minced

1 can (about 14 ounces) fire-roasted diced tomatoes

$3/4$ cup chunky salsa

2 teaspoons chili powder

1 teaspoon dried oregano

$1/2$ teaspoon salt

$1/4$ teaspoon black pepper

1 can (about 15 ounces) red kidney beans, rinsed and drained

1 package (14 to 16 ounces) extra firm tofu, drained and cut into $1/2$-inch cubes

Chopped fresh cilantro (optional)

LENTIL AND PORTOBELLO SOUP

MAKES 6 SERVINGS

1. Remove stems from mushrooms; coarsely chop stems. Cut caps into $\frac{1}{2}$-inch pieces.

2. Heat oil in large skillet over medium heat. Add onion, carrots and garlic; cook and stir 5 minutes or until onion is softened. Stir in lentils, tomatoes, broth, water, mushroom caps and stems, rosemary and bay leaf; season with salt and pepper.

3. Bring to a boil. Reduce heat to medium-low; simmer 20 to 25 minutes or until lentils are tender.

2 portobello mushrooms (about 8 ounces total), cleaned

1 tablespoon olive oil

1 onion, chopped

2 carrots, cut into $\frac{1}{4}$-inch-thick rounds

2 cloves garlic, minced

1 cup dried lentils, rinsed and sorted

1 can (28 ounces) diced tomatoes

1 can (about 14 ounces) vegetable broth

1 cup water

1 teaspoon dried rosemary

1 bay leaf

Salt and black pepper

SWEET POTATO, SQUASH AND CHICKPEA STEW

MAKES 6 SERVINGS

1. Heat oil in Dutch oven or large saucepan over medium heat. Add zucchini, eggplant, sweet potato and squash; cook and stir 8 to 10 minutes or until vegetables are slightly softened. Stir in tomatoes, chickpeas, raisins, cinnamon, orange peel, salt, cumin, paprika, red pepper and cardamom; bring to a boil over high heat.

2. Reduce heat to low; cover and simmer 30 minutes or until vegetables are tender. If sauce becomes too thick, stir in water to thin. Serve over couscous, if desired.

1/4 cup olive oil

3 cups sliced zucchini

2 cups cubed peeled eggplant

2 cups sliced quartered peeled sweet potato

1 1/2 cups cubed peeled butternut squash

1 can (28 ounces) crushed tomatoes in purée

1 can (about 15 ounces) chickpeas, rinsed and drained

1/2 cup raisins or currants

1 1/2 teaspoons ground cinnamon

1 teaspoon grated orange peel

1 teaspoon salt

3/4 teaspoon ground cumin

1/2 teaspoon paprika

1/4 teaspoon ground red pepper

1/8 teaspoon ground cardamom

Hot cooked couscous or rice (optional)

LENTIL CHILI

MAKES 4 SERVINGS

1. Heat oil in large saucepan over medium heat. Add onion; cook and stir 5 minutes or until softened. Add garlic; cook and stir 1 minute. Stir in chili powder, cumin and salt; cook and stir 30 seconds.

2. Add broth, lentils and hot pepper sauce; bring to a boil over high heat. Reduce heat to low; simmer 15 minutes. Stir in squash and tomatoes; simmer 18 to 20 minutes or until lentils and squash are tender.

3. Ladle into bowls; top with cilantro and pepitas.

1 tablespoon canola oil

1 onion, chopped

4 cloves garlic, minced

1 tablespoon chili powder

1 teaspoon ground cumin

1 teaspoon salt

4 cups (32 ounces) vegetable broth

3/4 cup dried brown or green lentils, rinsed and sorted

2 teaspoons smoked chipotle hot pepper sauce

2 cups diced peeled butternut squash

1 can (about 14 ounces) diced tomatoes

1/4 cup chopped fresh cilantro

1/4 cup pepitas (raw pumpkin seeds)

SANDWICHES, TACOS & BURGERS

CAULIFLOWER TARTINE

MAKES 4 SERVINGS

1. Prepare Pickled Red Onions.

2. Heat oil in medium skillet over medium-high heat. Add cauliflower; cook and stir 5 minutes or until browned. Add garlic, cumin, salt and thyme; cook and stir 30 seconds. Add 2 tablespoons water; cook and stir 5 minutes or until water is absorbed and cauliflower is crisp-tender.

3. Spread mayonnaise and mustard over each slice of bread. Top with Brie, cauliflower, sprouts, pickled onions and pine nuts.

PICKLED RED ONIONS: Bring 1/4 cup water, 2 tablespoons sugar and 1 teaspoon salt to a simmer in small saucepan; cook and stir just until sugar and salt are dissolved. Pour into medium jar or bowl; stir in 1 cup thinly sliced red onion and 3/4 cup white vinegar. Add enough additional water to cover, if needed. Let stand until ready to use; onions can be made a few days in advance.

Pickled Red Onions (recipe follows)

1 tablespoon olive oil

2 cups thinly sliced cauliflower florets

1 clove garlic, minced

1/2 teaspoon cumin seeds

1/2 teaspoon salt

1/4 teaspoon dried thyme

Mayonnaise and Dijon mustard

4 large bread slices, toasted

8 ounces Brie cheese, thinly sliced

Sprouts

2 tablespoons pine nuts, toasted*

*Spread pine nuts in small heavy skillet. Cook over medium heat 2 minutes or until lightly browned, stirring frequently.

BEET AND WALNUT BURGERS

MAKES 8 BURGERS

1. Combine boiling water and flaxseed in small bowl; cool completely.

2. Heat 1 tablespoon oil in large skillet over medium-high heat. Add onion, mushrooms and garlic; cook and stir about 8 minutes or until vegetables are softened and mushrooms are browned. Remove from heat; stir in salt, thyme, paprika, cumin and pepper. Cool slightly.

3. Place oats in food processor; process until finely ground. Add walnuts; pulse until nuts are coarsely chopped. Transfer oats and walnuts to large bowl.

4. Grate beet on large holes of box grater. Place mushroom mixture and beet in food processor; pulse until finely chopped. Add beans; pulse just until blended, leaving beans chunky. Add to bowl with nuts. Add flaxseed mixture and soy sauce; mix well. Refrigerate at least 30 minutes.

5. Heat 1 tablespoon oil in large nonstick skillet over medium-high heat. Shape mixture by heaping 1/2-cupfuls into 1/2-inch patties; place in skillet. Cook 5 minutes per side or until well browned and heated through. Repeat with remaining 1 tablespoon oil and beet mixture. Serve burgers on buns with desired toppings.

TIPS: Grating raw beets can be very messy. To minimize beet splatter, place a large bowl in your sink and place the box grater in the bowl. Grate the beet directly into the bowl. You may also want to wear an apron to protect your clothes from any stray beet juice. To toast the walnuts for this recipe, cook them in a medium skillet over medium heat about 5 minutes or until lightly browned, stirring frequently.

6 tablespoons boiling water

2 tablespoons ground flaxseed

3 tablespoons olive oil, divided

1 onion, chopped

1 package (8 ounces) sliced mushrooms

3 cloves garlic, chopped

2 teaspoons salt

1 teaspoon dried thyme

1/2 teaspoon smoked paprika

1/2 teaspoon ground cumin

1/4 teaspoon black pepper

1/2 cup old-fashioned oats

1 1/2 cups walnuts, toasted

1 large beet (about 1 pound), peeled

1 can (about 15 ounces) cannellini beans, rinsed and drained

1 tablespoon soy sauce

Hamburger buns

Lettuce, sliced red onion, avocado and/ or sliced tomato

BBQ PORTOBELLOS

MAKES 4 SERVINGS

1. Preheat oven to 375°F. Line large rimmed baking sheet with parchment paper.

2. Combine salt, paprika, onion powder, garlic powder, cumin and pepper in small bowl. Scrape gills from mushrooms and remove any stem. Cut mushrooms into ½-inch slices; place in large bowl. Drizzle with 2 tablespoons oil; toss to coat. Add seasoning mixture; toss until well blended. Arrange slices in single layer on prepared baking sheet.

3. Bake 15 minutes. Turn and bake 5 minutes or until mushrooms are tender and have shrunken slightly.

4. Meanwhile, heat remaining 1 teaspoon oil in medium saucepan over medium-high heat. Add onion; cook and stir 5 minutes or until onion is very soft. Add ketchup, vinegar, mustard, brown sugar and soy sauce; mix well. Reduce heat to low; simmer 5 minutes. Stir in mushrooms; mix well. Serve mushrooms on buns with desired toppings.

- 1 teaspoon salt
- 1 teaspoon smoked paprika
- 1 teaspoon onion powder
- ½ teaspoon garlic powder
- ½ teaspoon ground cumin
- ½ teaspoon black pepper
- 4 portobello mushroom caps
- 2 tablespoons plus 1 teaspoon olive oil, divided
- ½ medium yellow onion, finely chopped
- ¼ cup ketchup
- 2 tablespoons cider vinegar
- 1 tablespoon Dijon mustard
- 1 tablespoon packed brown sugar
- 1 teaspoon soy sauce
- 4 hamburger buns

  Sliced dill pickles and/or shredded cabbage or lettuce

CAULIFLOWER, WALNUT AND GRAPE SALAD
MAKES 6 SERVINGS

1. Preheat oven to 425°F. Place cauliflower on large rimmed baking sheet. Drizzle with oil and sprinkle with $1/2$ teaspoon salt and pepper; toss to coat. Roast 30 to 45 minutes or until cauliflower is very tender and desired degree of brownness. Cool completely.

2. Whisk mayonnaise, sour cream, vinegar, mustard and remaining $1/4$ teaspoon salt in large bowl. Stir in grapes, chives and cauliflower. Fold in walnuts. Serve in pita bread with lettuce.

1 large head cauliflower ($2^{1}/_{2}$ pounds), cut into 1-inch florets

2 tablespoons olive oil

$3/4$ teaspoon salt, divided

$1/4$ teaspoon black pepper

$1/2$ cup vegan or regular mayonnaise

$1/4$ cup vegan sour cream or plain Greek yogurt

1 teaspoon cider vinegar

1 teaspoon Dijon mustard

1 cup red grapes, halved

2 tablespoons minced fresh chives

$1/2$ cup chopped walnuts, toasted*

Pita bread, halved

Lettuce or baby spinach

*To toast walnuts, spread in medium skillet. Cook over medium heat 2 to 4 minutes or until lightly browned and fragrant, stirring frequently.

MINI BLACK BEAN PATTIES

MAKES 4 SERVINGS

1. Line cutting board or small baking sheet with parchment paper or waxed paper.

2. Heat 2 teaspoons oil in large nonstick skillet over medium-high heat. Add mushrooms, onion and garlic; cook and stir 5 minutes or until vegetables are tender. Transfer to food processor or blender. Add beans, oats, mayonnaise, thyme, salt and pepper. Pulse until mixture is finely minced but not pasty.

3. Shape mixture into eight 2-inch patties. Place on prepared cutting board; refrigerate 30 minutes.

4. Meanwhile for sauce, combine 2 tablespoons mayonnaise, yogurt and chives in small bowl. Refrigerate until ready to serve.

5. Heat remaining 2 teaspoons oil in large nonstick skillet over medium-high heat. Add burgers in single layer; cook about 5 minutes per side or until well browned and heated through. Serve on rolls, if desired, with chive sauce.

4 teaspoons vegetable or olive oil, divided

1 cup sliced cremini mushrooms

$1/2$ cup finely chopped onion

1 clove garlic, minced

1 can (about 15 ounces) black beans, drained

$1/4$ cup old-fashioned oats

2 tablespoons regular or vegan mayonnaise

$1/2$ teaspoon dried thyme

$1/4$ teaspoon salt

$1/4$ teaspoon black pepper

Slider rolls, dinner rolls or mini ($4^{1}/_{2}$-inch) tortillas (optional)

CHIVE SAUCE

2 tablespoons regular or vegan mayonnaise

2 tablespoons plain yogurt or vegan sour cream

1 tablespoon minced fresh chives

EGGPLANT BURGERS
MAKES 4 SERVINGS

1. Preheat oven to 375°F. Spray large rimmed baking sheet with nonstick cooking spray. Cut four ½-inch-thick slices from widest part of eggplant. Beat egg whites in shallow bowl. Place panko on medium plate.

2. Dip eggplant slices in egg whites. Place on panko; turn to coat both sides and press gently to adhere. Place on prepared baking sheet. Drizzle with 1 tablespoon oil. Bake 15 minutes or until golden brown. Turn eggplant and drizzle with remaining 1 tablespoon oil. Bake 15 minutes.

3. Spread mayonnaise on bottom halves of buns; top with spinach, tomatoes and eggplant. Top with cheese, if desired, and tops of buns.

1 eggplant (1¼ pounds), peeled

2 egg whites

½ cup panko bread crumbs

2 tablespoons olive oil, divided

3 tablespoons chipotle mayonnaise*

4 whole wheat hamburger buns

Baby spinach and thin tomato slices

4 slices pepper jack cheese (optional)

To make chipotle mayonnaise, stir enough chipotle chili powder or minced canned chipotle peppers into mayonnaise to reach your desired level of flavor and heat.

VEGETABLE FAJITAS WITH SPICY SALSA

MAKES 6 SERVINGS

1. For salsa, preheat broiler. Line baking sheet with parchment paper or foil. Place tomatoes, onion, jalapeño pepper and garlic on prepared baking sheet and broil 10 minutes. Turn vegetables and rotate pan. Broil 10 minutes or until blackened. Cool 10 minutes. Peel tomatoes, onion and garlic; peel and seed jalapeño pepper. Place in blender or food processor with lime juice and salt; process until desired consistency. Refrigerate until ready to use. (Can be made up to 1 week in advance.)

2. For fajitas, heat large cast iron or heavy skillet over medium-high heat. Cook tortillas in skillet one at a time until blistered and browned, about 15 seconds per side; stack and wrap in clean kitchen towel to keep warm.

3. Reduce heat to medium. Add oil; heat 30 seconds. Add bell pepper and red onion; sprinkle with salt and black pepper, if desired. Cook 10 minutes or until bell peppers are crisp-tender, stirring occasionally.

4. Prepare Avocado Spread, if desired. Spread about 2 tablespoons beans on each tortilla; spread some of avocado spread over beans. Top with vegetables and salsa. Roll up; serve immediately. Garnish with cilantro.

AVOCADO SPREAD: Scoop 2 avocados into a medium bowl, season with a generous pinch of salt and a squeeze of lime juice and mash it to a chunky but spreadable consistency. This spread is also delicious on any vegetable sandwich or burger, and makes a quick and easy topping for toast.

SALSA

- 3 medium tomatoes
- 1 yellow onion (unpeeled)
- 1 jalapeño pepper
- 6 cloves garlic (unpeeled)

  Juice of 1 lime
- 1 teaspoon salt

FAJITAS

- 12 (10-inch) flour tortillas
- 1 tablespoon canola oil
- 4 bell peppers, cut into strips
- 1 red onion, halved and thickly sliced
- 1 teaspoon salt

  Black pepper (optional)
- 1 can (about 15 ounces) vegetarian refried beans, warmed

  Avocado Spread (recipe follows, optional)

  Chopped fresh cilantro (optional)

SPROUTS AND BULGUR SANDWICHES

MAKES 4 SERVINGS

1. Rinse bulgur under cold running water; drain. Bring 1 cup water to a boil in small saucepan over high heat. Stir in bulgur. Remove from heat. Let stand, uncovered, 20 minutes. Drain well; squeeze out excess liquid.

2. Combine yogurt, mayonnaise and curry powder in medium bowl. Stir in bulgur, carrots, apple and peanuts. Taste and season with salt and black pepper.

3. Arrange sprouts on 4 slices of bread. Spread with bulgur mixture and top with remaining bread slices.

TIP: You could also try this sandwich with 1 cup cooked quinoa instead of the bulgur. To make it vegan, simply substitute vegan sour cream and mayonnaise for the regular versions.

$\frac{1}{2}$ cup bulgur wheat

1 cup water

$\frac{1}{2}$ cup plain yogurt or sour cream

$\frac{1}{4}$ cup mayonnaise

$1\frac{1}{2}$ teaspoons curry powder

1 cup shredded carrots

$\frac{1}{2}$ cup chopped apple

$\frac{1}{3}$ cup coarsely chopped peanuts

Salt and black pepper

2 cups sprouts

8 slices wheat bread, toasted

LENTIL SLOPPY JOES

MAKES 6 SERVINGS

1. Heat oil in medium saucepan over medium-high heat. Add onion and bell pepper; cook and stir 5 minutes or until onion is softened. Add sugar, chili powder, salt, garlic powder and onion powder; cook and stir 30 seconds. Stir in tomato sauce, lentils and broth; bring to a boil.

2. Reduce heat to low; simmer 30 to 40 minutes or until lentils are tender. Serve on buns with desired toppings.

1 tablespoon olive oil

1 onion, chopped

1 red or green bell pepper, chopped

3 tablespoons sugar

1 tablespoon chili powder

1 teaspoon salt

1/2 teaspoon garlic powder

1/2 teaspoon onion powder

1 can (about 15 ounces) tomato sauce

1 cup dried lentils, rinsed and sorted

1 cup vegetable broth

Hamburger buns, toasted

Optional toppings: avocado slices, onion slices and/or pickles

SWEET POTATO AND BLACK BEAN TACOS

MAKES 4 SERVINGS

1. Combine sour cream, mayonnaise, lime juice and chili powder in small bowl; mix well. Refrigerate until ready to use.

2. Combine beans with liquid and paprika in small saucepan. Cook over medium-low heat 5 to 7 minutes or until heated through, stirring occasionally. Remove from heat; coarsely mash beans with potato masher, leaving some beans whole. Keep warm.

3. Spiral sweet potato with medium spiral blade of spiralizer; cut into desired lengths. Or cut sweet potato into thin sticks or small cubes.

4. Heat 2 teaspoons oil in medium nonstick skillet over medium heat. Add sweet potato; cook and stir 7 to 10 minutes or until tender. Sprinkle with ¼ teaspoon salt.

5. Heat remaining 2 teaspoons oil in large nonstick skillet over high heat. Add onion and bell pepper; cook and stir 5 minutes or until vegetables are browned and softened. Sprinkle with remaining ¼ teaspoon salt.

6. Spread beans down middle of tortillas. Top with sweet potatoes, vegetables, sour cream mixture, avocado, cilantro and cheese, if desired; fold in half.

¼ cup sour cream

2 tablespoons mayonnaise

Juice of 1 lime

½ teaspoon chipotle chili powder

1 can (about 15 ounces) black beans, undrained

1 teaspoon smoked paprika

1 sweet potato, peeled and halved

4 teaspoons vegetable oil, divided

½ teaspoon salt, divided

1 red onion, thinly sliced

1 green bell pepper, thinly sliced

Small taco-size white corn tortillas

1 avocado, sliced

¼ cup chopped fresh cilantro

¼ cup grated cotija or Parmesan cheese (optional)

ENTRÉES & BOWLS

LENTILS WITH PASTA

MAKES 6 TO 8 SERVINGS

1. Place lentils and split peas in medium bowl; cover with water. Let stand at least 10 minutes.

2. Heat oil in large saucepan or Dutch oven over medium-high heat. Add onion; cook and stir 5 minutes or until onion is softened. Add tomato paste, garlic, salt and pepper; cook and stir 1 minute. Add tomatoes and 3 cups water; bring to a boil.

3. Drain lentils and split peas and add to saucepan. Reduce heat to medium-low; cover and simmer about 40 minutes or until lentils and split peas are tender.

4. Meanwhile, cook pasta in large saucepan of boiling salted water according to package directions for al dente. Drain and add to lentil mixture; mix well. Garnish with parsley.

1 cup dried lentils, rinsed and sorted

1 cup dried split peas

1 tablespoon olive oil

1 onion, chopped

2 tablespoons tomato paste

2 cloves garlic, minced

1 teaspoon salt

¼ teaspoon black pepper

1 can (about 14 ounces) diced tomatoes

3 cups water

12 ounces uncooked short pasta (small shells, elbow macaroni, ditalini or similar)

Minced fresh parsley

GINGER TOFU BOWL

MAKES 4 SERVINGS

1. Combine 6 tablespoons soy sauce, ginger and sesame oil in large resealable food storage bag or large bowl. Add tofu; seal bag and turn to coat. Refrigerate 2 hours or overnight.

2. Prepare rice according to package directions.

3. Meanwhile, place cucumber slices in shallow bowl. Sprinkle with salt and sugar; toss to coat. Add vinegar; mix well.

4. Heat vegetable oil in medium skillet over medium-high heat. Add mushrooms; cook and stir 5 minutes or until mushrooms are tender and lightly browned. Remove from heat; stir in remaining 1 tablespoon soy sauce.

5. Divide rice among four bowls. Drain tofu, discarding marinade. Arrange tofu, mushrooms, cucumbers, edamame and carrots over rice. Top with green onions, sesame seeds and pickled ginger.

NOTE: This is a great recipe to pack for lunches. Instead of plating all of the components in bowls in step 5, pack individual servings in food storage containers.

7 tablespoons soy sauce, divided

2 teaspoons minced fresh ginger

1 teaspoon toasted sesame oil

1 package (14 to 16 ounces) firm tofu, drained and cut into $1/2$-inch cubes

1 cup uncooked brown rice

$1/2$ seedless cucumber, thinly sliced

$1/4$ teaspoon salt

$1/4$ teaspoon sugar

$1/4$ cup rice vinegar

1 teaspoon vegetable oil

1 package (8 ounces) sliced cremini or white mushrooms

1 cup thawed frozen shelled edamame

2 carrots, julienned or thinly sliced

4 green onions, thinly sliced

Toasted sesame seeds and pickled ginger

HUMMUS VEGGIE BOWL
MAKES 4 SERVINGS

1. Whisk vinegar, sugar, 1/2 teaspoon salt and pepper in medium bowl. Stir in beets; let stand while preparing remaining ingredients.

2. Bring large saucepan of water to a boil. Add broccolini; cook 3 minutes. Drain and rinse under cold water to stop cooking.

3. For hummus and sauce, combine tahini, water, lemon juice, garlic and remaining 1 teaspoon salt in food processor; process until very smooth. Remove 1/2 cup to another medium bowl for sauce; whisk in enough additional water by teaspoonfuls until sauce is desired consistency.

4. Add chickpeas to food processor; process 5 minutes until hummus is fluffy and very smooth.

5. Spread some hummus in each of four serving bowls. Top with rice, if desired, beets, broccolini, avocados, carrots, green olives, if desired, and sauce.

TIP: To turn this bowl into an appetizer platter, cut the broccolini stalks in half lengthwise to make portions that are easier to snack on, or substitute broccoli instead. Cut the carrots and beets into sticks instead of julienne slices and substitute a cucumber, cut into slices or sticks, for the avocados. Place the hummus and tahini sauces in separate bowls and arrange the vegetables around them for dipping.

3 tablespoons white wine vinegar

1 teaspoon sugar

1 1/2 teaspoons salt, divided

1/8 teaspoon black pepper

1 large or 2 small beets, peeled and julienned*

1 to 2 bunches broccolini, stems trimmed 1/2 inch

1 1/4 cups tahini

6 tablespoons cold water

6 tablespoons lemon juice

1 clove garlic

1 can (30 ounces) chickpeas, drained

3 cups hot cooked rice (optional)

2 avocados, sliced

2 carrots, julienned*

Pitted green olives and/or sliced radishes (optional)

*Or shred on the large holes of a box grater.

SOBA TERIYAKI BOWL
MAKES 4 SERVINGS

1. Preheat oven to 400°F. Spray sheet pan with nonstick cooking spray. Whisk ³/₄ cup cornstarch and 1 teaspoon salt in medium bowl. Whisk in ¹/₂ cup water until smooth. Dip cauliflower into mixture; place in single layer on prepared sheet pan. Bake 20 minutes or until tender.

2. Meanwhile, combine pineapple juice, soy sauce, brown sugar, lime juice and garlic in small saucepan. Bring to a simmer over medium heat. Whisk 2 tablespoons water into remaining 1 tablespoon cornstarch in small bowl; stir into sauce. Reduce heat to low; cook and stir 5 minutes or until thickened. Transfer to large bowl; cool slightly. Remove ¹/₄ cup sauce to small bowl; set aside.

3. Cook soba noodles according to package directions. Drain and rinse under cold water until cool. Divide among four serving bowls.

4. Combine cabbage, vinegar, granulated sugar and remaining 1 teaspoon salt in medium bowl; mix and squeeze with hands until well blended.

5. Add cauliflower to large bowl of sauce; stir to coat. Divide among serving bowls. Drizzle some of reserved sauce over noodles. Serve with cabbage mixture. Sprinkle with green onions and sesame seeds.

³/₄ cup plus 1 tablespoon cornstarch, divided

2 teaspoons salt, divided

¹/₂ cup plus 2 tablespoons water, divided

1 head cauliflower, cut into 1-inch florets

³/₄ cup pineapple juice

³/₄ cup soy sauce

2 tablespoons packed brown sugar

1 tablespoon lime juice

1 teaspoon minced garlic

6 ounces uncooked soba noodles

5 cups shredded green and/or red cabbage or 1 package (14 ounces) coleslaw mix

¹/₂ cup unseasoned rice vinegar

1 teaspoon granulated sugar

2 green onions, chopped

1 tablespoon sesame seeds

MUJADARA

MAKES 4 TO 6 SERVINGS

1. Place lentils in medium saucepan; cover with water by 1 inch. Bring to a boil over medium-high heat. Reduce heat to medium-low; simmer 10 minutes. Drain and rinse under cold water.

2. Meanwhile, heat 1/4 cup oil in large saucepan or Dutch oven. Add onions and 1 teaspoon salt; cook and stir 15 minutes or until golden and parts are crispy. Remove most of onions to small bowl, leaving about 1/2 cup in saucepan.*

3. Add remaining 1 tablespoon oil to saucepan with onions; heat over medium-high heat. Add cumin, allspice, cinnamon stick, bay leaf and red pepper; cook and stir 30 seconds. Add rice; cook and stir 2 to 3 minutes or until rice is lightly toasted. Add broth, lentils and 1 teaspoon salt; bring to a boil. Reduce heat to low; cover and cook about 15 minutes or until broth is absorbed and rice and lentils are tender. Remove from heat. Place clean kitchen towel over top of saucepan; replace lid and let stand 5 to 10 minutes.

4. Meanwhile, peel cucumber and trim ends. Grate cucumber on large holes of box grater; squeeze out excess liquid. Place in medium bowl; stir in yogurt and remaining 1/2 teaspoon salt. Serve lentils and rice with reserved onions and cucumber sauce.

*If desired, continue to cook reserved onions in a medium skillet over medium heat until dark golden brown.

- 1 cup dried lentils, rinsed and sorted
- 1/4 cup plus 1 tablespoon olive oil, divided
- 3 sweet onions, thinly sliced
- 2 1/2 teaspoons salt, divided
- 1 1/2 teaspoons ground cumin
- 1 teaspoon ground allspice
- 1 cinnamon stick
- 1 bay leaf
- 1/8 to 1/4 teaspoon ground red pepper
- 3/4 cup long grain white rice, rinsed and drained
- 3 cups vegetable broth or water
- 1 cucumber
- 1 cup plain Greek yogurt or sour cream

LEMON CREAM PASTA WITH ROASTED CAULIFLOWER

MAKES 6 TO 8 SERVINGS

1. Preheat oven to 425°F. Place cauliflower on large rimmed baking sheet. Drizzle with oil and sprinkle with 1/2 teaspoon salt and 1/4 teaspoon black pepper; toss to coat. Roast 30 to 45 minutes or until cauliflower is tender and desired degree of brownness.

2. Cook pasta in large saucepan of boiling salted water according to package directions for al dente. Drain, reserving 1 cup pasta cooking water. Place pasta in large bowl; add cauliflower.

3. Melt butter in same saucepan over medium heat; whisk in flour until smooth paste forms. Whisk in milk, remaining 1/2 teaspoon salt and 1/8 teaspoon black pepper; cook and stir 2 to 3 minutes or until thickened. Whisk in 1/2 cup reserved pasta water and Parmesan until smooth.

4. Pour over pasta and cauliflower; stir to coat. Add additional pasta water by tablespoonfuls to loosen sauce, if needed. Stir in lemon juice, lemon peel and almonds. Top with arugula or gently fold into pasta mixture. Sprinkle with Aleppo pepper.

1 large head cauliflower (2 1/2 pounds), cut into 1-inch florets

2 tablespoons olive oil

1 teaspoon salt, divided

1/4 teaspoon plus 1/8 teaspoon black pepper, divided

8 ounces uncooked cavatappi pasta

1/4 cup (1/2 stick) butter, cut into pieces

1/4 cup all-purpose flour

2 cups milk

1/2 cup shredded Parmesan cheese

Grated peel and juice of 1 lemon

1/4 cup chopped almonds, toasted*

Baby arugula

Aleppo pepper or red pepper flakes (optional)

*To toast almonds, cook in medium skillet over medium heat 3 to 4 minutes or until lightly browned, stirring frequently.

SWEET POTATO MAKI BOWL

MAKES 4 SERVINGS

1. Preheat oven to 400°F. Line large rimmed baking sheet with foil; brush with 1 tablespoon oil.

2. Peel sweet potato and cut in half lengthwise; cut crosswise into ¼-inch slices. Combine panko, ¼ teaspoon salt and red pepper in shallow bowl. Combine ⅓ cup water, cornstarch and remaining ¼ teaspoon salt in another shallow bowl; mix until smooth. Dip sweet potato slices in cornstarch mixture, letting excess drip back into bowl. Roll in panko mixture to coat; place on prepared baking sheet.

3. Bake 20 to 25 minutes or until sweet potatoes are tender and topping is golden brown, turning once.

4. Meanwhile, cook rice according to package directions. Stir vinegar and granulated sugar into cooked rice.

5. Combine soy sauce and brown sugar in small saucepan; cook over low heat until mixture is reduced and syrupy. Combine mayonnaise and sriracha in small bowl, if desired.

6. Divide rice among four bowls. Top with sweet potatoes, cucumbers and avocado; drizzle with soy sauce mixture and sprinkle with sesame seeds. Serve with sriracha mayonnaise, if desired.

NOTE: Bowls are a lot of work but they pay off big in the end. You get a ton of textures and flavors, plus packable leftovers! And since each bowl is composed individually they are easy to customize to please picky eaters.

2 **tablespoons canola oil, divided**

1 **large sweet potato (about 18 ounces)**

½ **cup panko bread crumbs**

½ **teaspoon salt, divided**

⅛ **teaspoon ground red pepper**

⅓ **cup water**

¼ **cup cornstarch**

1 **cup Calrose rice, sushi rice or other short grain rice**

1 **tablespoon rice vinegar**

1 **teaspoon granulated sugar**

½ **cup soy sauce**

1 **tablespoon packed brown sugar**

¼ **cup vegan or regular mayonnaise (optional)**

1 **tablespoon sriracha sauce (optional)**

½ **cucumber, cut in half lengthwise and thinly sliced**

1 **avocado, cubed or sliced**

Sesame seeds

GREEK SALAD BOWL WITH FARRO AND CHICKPEAS

MAKES 4 SERVINGS

1. Rinse farro under cold running water; place in medium saucepan. Add 2½ cups water, 1 teaspoon oregano and ¼ teaspoon salt. Bring to a boil over high heat. Reduce heat to medium-low; simmer, uncovered, 20 minutes or until farro is tender. Drain any additional water.

2. For dressing, whisk oil, vinegar, garlic, remaining ¼ teaspoon salt, remaining ¼ teaspoon oregano and pepper in small bowl.

3. Divide farro among four bowls; arrange cucumbers, onion, tomatoes, chickpeas and feta around farro. Drizzle with dressing.

NOTE: This is a great recipe to use a spiralizer if you have one. Cut the ends off the cucumbers and spiral slice with the thin ribbon blade. Spiral the red onion with the thin ribbon blade and chop into desired pieces.

1 cup uncooked pearled farro

2½ cups water

1¼ teaspoons dried oregano or Greek seasoning, divided

½ teaspoon salt, divided

¼ cup olive oil

2 tablespoons red wine vinegar

1 clove garlic, minced

⅛ teaspoon black pepper

2 cucumbers, julienned, diced or thinly sliced

½ red onion, thinly sliced

2 medium tomatoes, diced

1 can (about 15 ounces) chickpeas, rinsed and drained

4 ounces feta cheese, cubed or crumbled

TUSCAN KALAMATA OLIVE AND WHITE BEAN PASTA

MAKES 4 SERVINGS

1. Combine oil, garlic, salt and red pepper flakes in small bowl; set aside.

2. Cook pasta according to package directions in large saucepan of boiling salted water for al dente. Meanwhile, drain beans and tomatoes in large colander. Pour pasta and cooking water over beans and tomatoes in colander. Drain well. Transfer to large bowl.

3. Add garlic mixture, spinach, olives, pine nuts and basil. Toss gently to blend well. Top with feta cheese, if desired.

2 tablespoons olive oil

1 clove garlic, minced

1/2 teaspoon salt

1/8 teaspoon red pepper flakes

8 ounces uncooked rotini pasta

1 can (about 15 ounces) navy beans

1 can (about 14 ounces) diced tomatoes

1 cup packed baby spinach, coarsely chopped

1/2 cup halved pitted kalamata olives

1/4 cup pine nuts, toasted*

2 tablespoons chopped fresh basil

2 ounces crumbled feta cheese (optional)

*To toast pine nuts, spread in single layer in small skillet. Cook over medium heat 1 to 2 minutes until nuts are lightly browned, stirring frequently.

SESAME GINGER-GLAZED TOFU WITH RICE

MAKES 4 SERVINGS

1. Slice tofu in half crosswise. Cut each half into 2 triangles. Place tofu triangles on cutting board between layers of paper towels. Place another cutting board on top to press moisture out of tofu. Let stand about 15 minutes.

2. Meanwhile for sauce, combine soy sauce, brown sugar, water, sesame oil, vinegar, ginger, garlic and red pepper flakes, if desired, in medium bowl. Pour 1/2 cup sauce in baking dish. Place tofu in sauce; marinate at room temperature 30 minutes, turning after 15 minutes.

3. Cook rice according to package directions.

4. Spray grill pan or large nonstick skillet with nonstick cooking spray; heat over medium-high heat. Add tofu; cook 6 to 8 minutes or until lightly browned, turning after 4 minutes.

5. Meanwhile, heat vegetable oil in large nonstick skillet over medium-high heat. Add carrots and snow peas; cook and stir 4 to 6 minutes or until crisp-tender. Stir in rice and remaining sauce until well blended. Serve with tofu.

1 package (14 to 16 ounces) firm or extra firm tofu

6 tablespoons soy sauce

3 tablespoons packed brown sugar

3 tablespoons water

3 tablespoons toasted sesame oil

2 tablespoons rice vinegar

2 tablespoons grated fresh ginger

1 clove garlic, minced

1/4 teaspoon red pepper flakes (optional)

1 cup uncooked long grain rice

2 teaspoons vegetable oil

2 carrots, chopped (about 1 cup)

4 ounces snow peas, halved (about 1 cup)

SPAGHETTI WITH FRESH TOMATO-OLIVE SAUCE

MAKES 4 TO 6 SERVINGS

1. Combine tomatoes, onion, parsley, olives, garlic, basil, capers, paprika and oregano in medium bowl; mix well. Drizzle with vinegar. Add oil; stir until well blended. Season to taste with salt and pepper. Cover and let stand at room temperature 2 to 6 hours.

2. Cook pasta in large saucepan of boiling salted water according to package directions for al dente; drain. Toss hot pasta with tomato sauce. Serve immediately.

1 pound plum tomatoes, coarsely chopped

1 medium onion, chopped

1/3 cup chopped fresh parsley

6 pitted green olives, chopped

2 cloves garlic, minced

2 tablespoons finely shredded fresh basil

2 teaspoons drained capers

1/2 teaspoon paprika

1/4 teaspoon dried oregano

1 tablespoon red wine vinegar

1/2 cup olive oil

Salt and black pepper

1 pound uncooked spaghetti

SIZZLING CRÊPES (BAHN XEO)

MAKES 4 SERVINGS

1. Combine rice flour, salt, $1/2$ teaspoon sugar and turmeric in medium bowl. Gradually whisk in coconut milk and $1/2$ cup water until batter is thickness of heavy cream. Let batter rest at least 10 minutes. Add additional water as needed to thin batter.

2. Heat 9- or 10-inch nonstick skillet over medium heat. Add 1 tablespoon oil to skillet. Add one fourth of tofu and 1 tablespoon green onions; cook and stir 2 to 4 minutes or until onions are softened and tofu is lightly browned.

3. Pour about $1/2$ cup batter over fillings. Immediately swirl to coat bottom of skillet with batter; allow some batter to go up side of skillet. In 30 seconds or when sizzling sound stops, add bean sprouts to one side of crêpe. Cover skillet and cook 3 minutes or until sprouts wilt, center of crêpe appears cooked and edge is browned and crisp. Fold crêpe in half with spatula and transfer to plate. Repeat with remaining oil, fillings and batter.

4. For dipping sauce, stir $2/3$ cup water, soy sauce, 2 tablespoons sugar and lime juice in small bowl until sugar dissolves. Stir in garlic and serrano pepper.

5. Serve crêpes with lettuce, bell pepper, carrots, herbs and dipping sauce. Traditionally, crêpes are eaten by wrapping bite-size portions in lettuce with herbs and dipping each bite in sauce.

NOTE: Sizzling crêpes (Banh Xeo, pronounced bahn SAY-oh) are a popular Vietnamese street snack. The word "Xeo" in Vietnamese mimics the sound the batter makes as it sizzles in the pan.

CRÊPES

- 1 cup rice flour
- $1/2$ teaspoon salt
- $1/2$ teaspoon sugar
- $1/2$ teaspoon turmeric
- 1 cup unsweetened coconut milk
- $1/2$ to $3/4$ cup water

FILLING

- $1/4$ cup vegetable oil, divided
- 1 package (14 to 16 ounces) firm tofu, drained and cubed
- $1/4$ cup chopped green onions
- 2 cups bean sprouts

  Lettuce, sliced bell pepper and carrots, fresh cilantro and fresh mint

DIPPING SAUCE

- $2/3$ cup water
- $1/4$ cup soy sauce
- 2 tablespoons sugar

  Juice of 1 lime
- 1 clove garlic, minced
- 1 serrano or other hot pepper, minced

VEGGIE "MEATBALLS"

MAKES 4 SERVINGS

1. Preheat oven to 375°F. Line large rimmed baking sheet with foil; spray with nonstick cooking spray.

2. Bring water to a boil in small saucepan; remove from heat. Stir in bulgur; cover and let stand while preparing vegetables.

3. Heat oil in large skillet over medium-high heat. Add mushrooms, onion, zucchini, Italian seasoning and salt; cook and stir about 8 minutes or until softened. Add garlic; cook and stir 1 minute. Stir in tomatoes.

4. Transfer mushroom mixture to large bowl; cool slightly. Add bulgur, Parmesan cheese and egg whites; mix well. Shape mixture into 12 balls using 1/4 cup for each. Place balls on prepared baking sheet.

5. Bake 20 minutes. Turn balls; bake 8 to 10 minutes or until well browned. Serve hot with marinara sauce.

1/2 cup water

3/4 cup bulgur wheat

2 teaspoons olive oil

3 medium portobello mushrooms, stemmed and diced

1 onion, chopped

1 small zucchini (6 ounces), grated on large holes of box grater

1 teaspoon Italian seasoning

1 teaspoon salt

2 cloves garlic, minced

1/4 cup sun-dried tomatoes (not packed in oil*), chopped

4 ounces grated Parmesan cheese

2 egg whites

2 cups marinara sauce, heated

*Or substitute 1/4 cup sun-dried tomatoes packed in oil, well drained, patted dry and chopped.

TOFU SOBA STIR-FRY

MAKES 4 SERVINGS

1. Bring 6 cups water to a boil in large saucepan. Add noodles. Boil 1 minute to soften. Rinse under cold water and drain.

2. Heat 1 tablespoon oil in large nonstick skillet over medium-high heat. Add tofu; cook until browned on all sides, turning occasionally. Transfer to plate. Add remaining 1 tablespoon oil to skillet. Add garlic and ginger. Cook and stir about 1 minute or until fragrant. Stir in water chestnuts and baby corn.

3. Return tofu to skillet. Add broth, soy sauce, snow peas and drained noodles; bring to a boil. Reduce heat; simmer 3 minutes or until noodles are tender and most of liquid is absorbed. Stir in green onions.

4 ounces uncooked soba noodles

2 tablespoons vegetable oil, divided

1 package (14 to 16 ounces) firm tofu, drained, cut into 1-inch cubes and patted dry

4 cloves garlic, minced

1 tablespoon minced fresh ginger

1 can (8 ounces) water chestnuts

1 cup baby corn

1 1/2 cups mushroom or vegetable broth

2 tablespoons soy sauce

1 cup snow peas

1/4 cup thinly sliced green onions

THAI VEGGIE CURRY

MAKES 4 TO 6 SERVINGS

1. Heat oil in large skillet or wok over medium-high heat. Add onion; cook and stir 2 minutes or until softened. Add curry paste; cook and stir to coat onion. Add coconut milk; bring to a boil, stirring to dissolve curry paste.

2. Reduce heat to medium. Add bell peppers and cauliflower; simmer 4 to 5 minutes or until crisp-tender. Stir in snow peas; simmer 2 minutes. Gently stir in tofu; cook until heated through. Season with salt and black pepper.

3. Sprinkle with basil; serve with rice.

2 tablespoons vegetable oil

1 onion, quartered and thinly sliced

2 tablespoons Thai red curry paste

1 can (14 ounces) unsweetened coconut milk

2 red or yellow bell peppers, cut into strips

1½ cups cauliflower and/or broccoli florets

1 cup snow peas

1 package (about 14 ounces) tofu, pressed and cubed

Salt and black pepper

¼ cup slivered fresh basil

Hot cooked jasmine rice

VEGETABLE
MAINS & SIDES

COUSCOUS PRIMAVERA

MAKES 2 TO 4 SERVINGS

1. Heat oil in large skillet over medium heat. Add shallot; cook and stir 3 minutes or until tender. Add asparagus and peas; cook and stir 2 minutes or until peas are heated through. Add tomatoes; cook 2 minutes or until softened. Add water, salt and pepper; bring to a boil.

2. Stir in couscous. Reduce heat to low. Cover; simmer 2 minutes or until liquid is absorbed. Fluff with fork. Stir in cheese just before serving, if desired.

2 teaspoons olive oil

1 shallot, minced *or* $1/4$ cup minced red onion

8 asparagus spears, cut into 1-inch pieces

1 cup frozen peas

1 cup halved grape tomatoes

$1/2$ cup water

$1/2$ teaspoon salt

$1/8$ teaspoon black pepper

6 tablespoons uncooked whole wheat couscous

$1/4$ cup shredded Parmesan cheese (optional)

ROASTED PEPPERS AND POTATOES
MAKES 4 TO 6 SERVINGS

1. Preheat oven to 375°F.

2. Place potatoes, bell peppers and onion in large bowl. Combine oil, garlic, salt, black pepper, basil and oregano in small bowl; pour over vegetables. Stir until vegetables are evenly coated. Spread on large rimmed baking sheet.

3. Bake 40 to 50 minutes or until potatoes are tender and well browned, stirring every 15 minutes.

NOTE: To give roasted vegetables a boost of flavor, try topping them with a zesty herb sauce like pesto or chimichurri sauce. Chimichurri is a traditional Argentinian sauce usually served on steak, but it is quite delicious on roasted vegetables like the ones in this recipe. To make it, place 1 cup packed fresh parsley, 1/2 cup packed fresh basil leaves, 1/4 cup packed fresh cilantro, 1 clove garlic, 1/2 teaspoon salt, 1/2 teaspoon grated lemon peel, 1/4 teaspoon ground coriander and 1/8 teaspoon black pepper in food processor or blender. Pulse until finely chopped. Transfer to a medium bowl; stir in 1/3 cup olive oil, 2 tablespoons lemon juice and 2 tablespoons red wine vinegar. Makes about 1 cup.

2 pounds small unpeeled red potatoes, quartered

1 large red bell pepper, cut into 1 1/2-inch pieces

1 large yellow or orange bell pepper, cut into 1 1/2-inch pieces

1 large red or sweet onion, cut into 1-inch pieces or wedges

1/4 cup olive oil

3 cloves garlic, minced

3/4 teaspoon salt

1/4 teaspoon black pepper

1/4 teaspoon dried basil

1/4 teaspoon dried oregano or thyme

ROASTED RAINBOW CARROTS WITH SWEET TAHINI

MAKES 4 SERVINGS

1. Preheat oven to 400°F. Place carrots on large rimmed baking sheet; drizzle with oil. Combine 1¹/₂ teaspoons salt, 1 teaspoon ground cumin, thyme and pepper in small bowl. Sprinkle over carrots; roll carrots to coat with oil and seasonings.

2. Roast 20 minutes or until carrots are fork-tender and slightly charred, turning once. Place on serving plate.

3. Meanwhile for sauce, whisk tahini, lemon juice, maple syrup, ¹/₄ teaspoon salt and dash of cumin in small bowl. Whisk in water until smooth. Pour over carrots.

CARROTS

- 2 pounds rainbow carrots, peeled and halved lengthwise if large
- ¹/₄ cup olive oil
- 1¹/₂ teaspoons salt
- 1 teaspoon ground cumin
- ¹/₂ teaspoon dried thyme
- ¹/₂ teaspoon black pepper, Aleppo pepper or red pepper flakes

SAUCE

- 2 tablespoons tahini
- 1 tablespoon lemon juice
- 1 tablespoon maple syrup
- ¹/₄ teaspoon salt
- Dash of ground cumin
- 2 tablespoons water

BALSAMIC BUTTERNUT SQUASH

MAKES 4 SERVINGS

1. Heat oil in large (12-inch) cast iron skillet over medium-high heat. Add 1 tablespoon sage; cook and stir 3 minutes. Add squash, onion and ½ teaspoon salt; cook 6 minutes, stirring occasionally. Reduce heat to medium; cook 15 minutes without stirring.

2. Stir in vinegar, remaining ½ teaspoon salt and pepper; cook 10 minutes or until squash is tender, stirring occasionally. Stir in remaining 1 tablespoon sage; cook 1 minute.

NOTE: Leftover squash is a great thing to have in your fridge. Add it to salads like French Lentil Salad on page 32 or Kale Salad with Cherries and Avocados on page 48. It also makes a great quesadilla filling. Mash it up with some black beans and chipotle chili powder and spread it on half of a flour tortilla. Sprinkle with some shredded melty cheese like chihuahua, Monterey Jack, Muenster or mozzarella if you're doing dairy, or add some pepitas and chopped fresh spinach if you're not, fold in half and cook in a hot skillet about 2 minutes per side or until heated through.

3 tablespoons olive oil

2 tablespoons thinly sliced fresh sage (about 6 large leaves), divided

1 medium butternut squash, peeled and cut into 1-inch pieces (4 to 5 cups)

½ red onion, halved and cut into ¼-inch slices

1 teaspoon salt, divided

2½ tablespoons balsamic vinegar

¼ teaspoon black pepper

QUINOA AND ROASTED CORN

MAKES 4 SERVINGS

1. Place quinoa in fine-mesh strainer; rinse well under cold running water. Combine quinoa, 2 cups water and 1/2 teaspoon salt in medium saucepan; bring to a boil over high heat. Reduce heat to low; cover and simmer 15 to 18 minutes or until quinoa is tender and water is absorbed. Transfer to large bowl.

2. Meanwhile, remove husks and silk from corn; cut kernels off cobs. Heat 1/4 cup oil in large skillet over medium-high heat. Add corn; cook 10 to 12 minutes or until tender and lightly browned, stirring occasionally. Stir in 2/3 cup green onions and remaining 1 teaspoon salt; cook and stir 2 minutes. Add corn mixture to quinoa. Gently stir in tomatoes and beans.

3. Combine lime juice, lime peel, sugar, cumin and pepper in small bowl. Whisk in remaining 1 tablespoon oil until blended. Pour over quinoa mixture; toss gently to blend. Sprinkle with remaining 1/3 cup green onions. Serve warm or cold.

- 1 cup uncooked quinoa
- 2 cups water
- 1 1/2 teaspoons salt, divided
- 4 ears corn *or* 2 cups frozen corn
- 1/4 cup plus 1 tablespoon vegetable oil, divided
- 1 cup chopped green onions, divided
- 1 cup quartered grape tomatoes or chopped plum tomatoes
- 1 cup canned black beans, rinsed and drained
- Juice of 1 lime (about 2 tablespoons)
- 1/4 teaspoon grated lime peel
- 1/4 teaspoon sugar
- 1/4 teaspoon ground cumin
- 1/4 teaspoon black pepper

MEXICAN CAULIFLOWER AND BEAN SKILLET

MAKES 4 TO 6 SERVINGS

1. Heat oil in large skillet over medium-high heat. Add cauliflower and salt; cook and stir 5 minutes. Add onion, bell pepper, garlic, chili powder, cumin and red pepper; cook and stir 5 minutes or until cauliflower is tender. Add beans; cook until beans are heated through. Remove from heat.

2. Sprinkle with cheese, if desired; fold gently and let stand until melted. Serve with salsa, if desired.

GUACAMOLE: Cut 2 large ripe avocados in half lengthwise around pits. Remove pits. Scoop avocados into large bowl; sprinkle with 2 teaspoons lime juice and toss to coat. Add 1/4 cup finely chopped red onion, 2 tablespoons chopped fresh cilantro, 2 tablespoons finely chopped jalapeño pepper and 1/2 teaspoon salt; stir gently until well blended. Taste and add additional salt, if desired. Makes 2 cups.

1 teaspoon olive oil

3 cups coarsely chopped cauliflower

3/4 teaspoon salt

1/2 medium onion, chopped

1 green bell pepper, chopped

1 clove garlic, minced

1 teaspoon chili powder

3/4 teaspoon ground cumin

Dash of ground red pepper

1 can (about 15 ounces) black beans, rinsed and drained

1 cup (4 ounces) shredded Cheddar-Jack cheese or vegan shredded cheese (optional)

Salsa and/or guacamole (optional)

MA PO TOFU

MAKES 4 SERVINGS

1. Cut tofu into cubes. Place in shallow dish; sprinkle with soy sauce and ginger.

2. Whisk ¼ cup broth, black bean sauce, chili sauce and cornstarch in small bowl until smooth and well blended; set aside.

3. Heat oil in wok or large skillet over high heat. Add bell pepper and garlic; stir-fry 2 minutes. Add remaining ¾ cup broth and broccoli; bring to a boil. Reduce heat; cover and simmer 3 minutes or until broccoli is crisp-tender.

4. Stir sauce mixture; add to wok. Stir-fry 1 minute or until sauce boils and thickens. Stir in tofu; simmer, uncovered, until heated through. Sprinkle with cilantro, if desired. Serve with rice.

1 package (14 to 16 ounces) firm tofu, drained and pressed*

2 tablespoons soy sauce

2 teaspoons minced fresh ginger

1 cup vegetable broth, divided

2 tablespoons black bean sauce

1 tablespoon Thai sweet chili sauce

1 tablespoon cornstarch

2 tablespoons vegetable oil

1 green bell pepper, cut into 1-inch pieces

2 cloves garlic, minced

1½ cups broccoli florets

¼ cup chopped fresh cilantro (optional)

Hot cooked rice

*Cut tofu in half horizontally and place it between layers of paper towels. Place a weighted cutting board on top; let stand 15 to 30 minutes.

WHOLE ROASTED CAULIFLOWER

MAKES 4 TO 6 SERVINGS

1. Preheat oven to 400°F. Line 13×9-inch baking pan with foil.

2. Rub 4 tablespoons oil all over cauliflower, 1 tablespoon at a time. Sprinkle with ½ teaspoon salt and season with black pepper. Place in prepared baking pan; add ¼ cup water to pan. Roast 45 minutes, adding additional water if pan is dry.

3. Combine panko, Parmesan, garlic, oregano, sage, red pepper flakes and remaining ⅛ teaspoon salt in small bowl. Stir in remaining 2 tablespoons oil. Remove pan from oven and carefully pat panko mixture all over and under cauliflower. Bake 15 minutes or until panko is browned and cauliflower is tender. Cut into wedges to serve.

NOTE: A whole roasted head of cauliflower makes an impressive presentation and is often the centerpiece of vegetarian Thanksgiving feasts. It also makes a good accompaniment to a simple pasta dish or a big salad for a weeknight meal.

6 tablespoons olive oil, divided

1 head cauliflower, leaves trimmed

½ teaspoon plus ⅛ teaspoon salt, divided

Black pepper

¾ cup panko bread crumbs

¼ cup shredded Parmesan cheese

1 clove garlic, minced

¼ teaspoon dried oregano

¼ teaspoon dried sage

⅛ teaspoon red pepper flakes

POTATO GNOCCHI WITH TOMATO SAUCE

MAKES 4 SERVINGS

1. For gnocchi, preheat oven to 425°F. Pierce potatoes with fork. Bake 1 hour or until soft.

2. Meanwhile for tomato sauce, heat oil in medium saucepan over medium heat. Add garlic; cook 30 seconds or until fragrant. Stir in tomatoes and sugar; cook 10 minutes or until most of liquid has evaporated, stirring occasionally. Stir in 1 tablespoon basil; cook 2 minutes. Season to taste with salt and pepper. Keep warm.

3. Cut potatoes in half lengthwise; cool slightly. Scoop out potatoes from skins into medium bowl; discard skins. Mash potatoes until smooth. Add $2/3$ cup flour, egg yolk, $1/2$ teaspoon salt and nutmeg, if desired; gently mix to form dough.

4. Turn out dough onto well-floured surface. Knead in enough remaining flour to form smooth dough (do not overwork dough or gnocchi will be tough). Divide dough into four pieces; roll each piece with hands on lightly floured surface into $3/4$- to 1-inch-wide rope. Cut each rope into 1-inch pieces; gently press thumb into center of each piece to make indentation. Transfer gnocchi to lightly floured kitchen towel in single layer.

5. Bring 4 quarts salted water to a gentle boil in large saucepan over high heat. To test cooking time, drop several gnocchi into water; cook 1 minute or until they float to surface. Remove from water with slotted spoon and taste for doneness. (If gnocchi start to dissolve, shorten cooking time by several seconds.) Cook remaining gnocchi in batches, removing with slotted spoon to serving dish. Serve with tomato sauce; sprinkle with slivered basil.

GNOCCHI

- 2 pounds baking potatoes (3 or 4 large)
- $2/3$ to 1 cup all-purpose flour, divided
- 1 egg yolk
- $1/2$ teaspoon salt
- $1/8$ teaspoon ground nutmeg (optional)
- Slivered fresh basil

TOMATO SAUCE

- 2 tablespoons olive oil
- 1 clove garlic, minced
- 2 pounds ripe plum tomatoes, peeled, seeded and chopped
- 1 teaspoon sugar
- 1 tablespoon finely chopped fresh basil
- Salt and black pepper

CORNMEAL-CRUSTED CAULIFLOWER STEAKS

MAKES 4 SERVINGS

1. Preheat oven to 400°F. Line baking sheet with parchment paper.

2. Combine cornmeal, flour, salt, sage and garlic powder in shallow bowl or baking pan. Season with pepper. Pour oat milk into another shallow bowl.

3. Turn cauliflower stem side up on cutting board. Trim away leaves, leaving stem intact. Slice through stem into 2 or 3 slices. Trim off excess florets from two end slices, creating flat "steaks." Repeat with remaining cauliflower; reserve extra cauliflower for another use.

4. Dip cauliflower in oat milk to coat both sides. Place in cornmeal mixture; pat onto all sides of cauliflower. Place on prepared baking sheet. Drizzle butter evenly over cauliflower.

5. Bake 40 minutes or until cauliflower is tender. Serve with barbecue sauce for dipping, if desired.

NOTE: These cauliflower steaks are perfect dipped in barbecue sauce, and nothing goes better with barbecue than coleslaw (try Pepita Lime Cabbage Slaw on page 30). Add a can of vegetarian baked beans to round out your veggie barbecue feast.

RANCH DRESSING: Combine ³/₄ cup buttermilk, ¹/₂ cup mayonnaise, ¹/₄ cup sour cream, 1 tablespoon lemon juice, 1 clove garlic, 1 tablespoon minced fresh chives, 1 tablespoon chopped fresh basil, 1 tablespoon minced fresh dill and ¹/₂ teaspoon salt in food processor or blender; process until combined. Makes about 2 cups.

¹/₂ cup cornmeal

¹/₄ cup all-purpose flour or cornstarch

1 teaspoon salt

1 teaspoon dried sage

¹/₂ teaspoon garlic powder

Black pepper

¹/₂ cup oat milk or regular milk

2 heads cauliflower

4 tablespoons vegan plant butter or regular butter, melted

Barbecue sauce or ranch dressing (optional)

GRILLED CORN AND BELL PEPPER KABOBS

MAKES 4 SERVINGS

1. Alternately thread corn, bell peppers and onion onto four 12-inch metal skewers. Brush oil evenly over vegetables. Combine seasoned salt, chili powder and sugar in small bowl; sprinkle over all sides of vegetables.

2. Prepare grill for direct cooking. Place skewers on grid over medium heat. Grill 10 to 12 minutes or until vegetables are tender, turning occasionally.

TIP: To prepare skewers ahead of time, wrap them up in foil after step 1 and refrigerate up to 8 hours.

4 ears corn, husked and cut into halves or thirds

1 red bell pepper, cut into 12 chunks

1 yellow bell pepper, cut into 12 chunks

1 green bell pepper, cut into 12 chunks

1 medium red or sweet onion, cut into 12 wedges

2 tablespoons olive oil

1 teaspoon seasoned salt or regular salt

1 teaspoon chili powder

$\frac{1}{2}$ teaspoon sugar

SUMMER SALAD LETTUCE WRAPS

MAKES 6 WRAPS

1. Whisk oil, lime juice and vinegar in large bowl.

2. Add tomatoes, corn, cheese, onion and basil; toss to coat. Season with salt and pepper.

3. To serve, scoop 1/4 cup salad mixture onto each lettuce leaf; fold or roll up.

1/4 cup olive oil

Juice of 1 lime

1 tablespoon red wine vinegar

1 cup grape tomatoes, halved

1 cup fresh corn

1/2 cup diced fresh mozzarella cheese

1/4 cup diced red onion

1/4 cup chopped fresh basil

Salt and black pepper

6 crunchy lettuce leaves

VEGETABLE TIAN
MAKES 4 TO 6 SERVINGS

1. Preheat oven to 350°F. Place 1 tablespoon oil in oval baking dish or 13×9-inch baking dish; tilt to coat bottom.

2. Cut tomatoes, onion, zucchini, eggplant, squash and mushroom into thin slices ($\frac{1}{8}$ to $\frac{1}{4}$ inch). Arrange vegetables in rows in prepared baking dish, alternating different types and overlapping slices in dish to make attractive arrangement; sprinkle evenly with garlic. Combine remaining 3 tablespoons oil and rosemary in small bowl; drizzle over vegetables.

3. Pour wine over vegetables; generously season with salt and pepper. Cover loosely with foil. Bake 20 minutes. Uncover; bake 15 to 20 minutes or until vegetables are tender.

TIP: Serve this hearty warming vegetable dish as a meal with a simple green salad and toasted slices of crusty bread. Turn leftovers into a sandwich or panini by layering leftover vegetables and cheese or hummus between slices of bread. Cook the sandwich in a hot skillet 3 minutes per side or until bread is toasted and filling is hot, or use a panini press.

4 tablespoons olive oil, divided

2 large tomatoes

1 small red onion

1 zucchini

1 small eggplant

1 yellow squash

1 large portobello mushroom

2 cloves garlic, finely chopped

2 teaspoons chopped fresh rosemary, thyme or oregano

$\frac{1}{4}$ cup dry white wine

Salt and black pepper

SNACKS & SMALL PLATES

GREEN BEAN FRIES

MAKES 4 TO 6 SERVINGS

1. Place flaxseed in small bowl; stir in boiling water. Refrigerate until cold.

2. Bring large saucepan of salted water to a boil. Add green beans; cook 4 minutes or until crisp-tender. Drain and rinse under cold running water to stop cooking.

3. Combine cornstarch and flour in large bowl. Whisk oat milk and flaxseed mixture in another large bowl. Combine bread crumbs, salt, onion powder and garlic powder in shallow bowl. Place green beans in flour mixture; toss to coat. Working in batches, coat beans with flaxseed mixture, letting excess drain back into bowl. Roll beans in bread crumb mixture to coat. Place on large baking sheet.

4. Place 3 inches of oil in large deep saucepan. Clip deep-fry or candy thermometer to side of pan. Heat over medium-high heat to 375°F; adjust heat to maintain temperature during frying. Cook green beans in batches about 1 minute or until golden brown. Drain on paper towel-lined plate.

1 tablespoon ground flaxseed

3 tablespoons boiling water

8 ounces fresh green beans, trimmed

1/2 cup cornstarch

1/4 cup all-purpose flour

3/4 cup oat milk

1 cup plain dry bread crumbs

1 teaspoon salt

1/2 teaspoon onion powder

1/4 teaspoon garlic powder

Vegetable oil for frying

VEGETABLE SUSHI

MAKES 6 SUSHI ROLLS (36 PIECES)

1. Combine rice and water in medium saucepan. Cover and bring to a boil. Reduce heat to very low. Cover and cook 15 to 20 minutes or until rice is tender and water is absorbed. Let stand, covered, 10 minutes.

2. Meanwhile, heat small nonstick skillet over medium heat. Add sesame oil and mushrooms; cook and stir 2 to 3 minutes or until tender. Wrap asparagus in plastic wrap and microwave 1 minute.

3. Spoon rice into shallow nonmetallic bowl. Sprinkle vinegar over rice and fold in gently with wooden spoon. Cut sheet of nori in half lengthwise, parallel to lines marked on rough side. Place lengthwise, shiny side down, on bamboo rolling mat or piece of plastic wrap.

4. Fill small bowl with water to rinse fingers and prevent rice from sticking while working. Spread about $1/2$ cup rice over nori, leaving $1/2$-inch border at top edge. Spread pinch of wasabi across center of rice. Arrange strips of 2 different vegetables over wasabi. Do not overfill.

5. Pick up edge of mat nearest you. Roll mat forward, wrapping rice around fillings and pressing gently to form log, or roll using plastic wrap as a guide. Once roll is formed, press gently to seal; place completed roll on cutting board, seam side down. Repeat with remaining nori, rice and vegetables.

6. Slice each roll into 6 pieces with sharp knife. Wipe knife with damp cloth between cuts. Arrange sushi on serving plates with pickled ginger, soy sauce and additional wasabi for dipping.

$1/4$ cups Japanese short grain sushi rice,* rinsed in several changes of water

$1/2$ cups water

1 teaspoon toasted sesame oil

4 medium shiitake mushrooms, thinly sliced

4 thin asparagus spears

$2^{1/2}$ tablespoons seasoned rice vinegar

3 sheets nori (from 0.6 ounce package)

Prepared wasabi

$1/2$ red bell pepper, cut into long, thin pieces

$1/2$ seedless cucumber, cut into long, thin pieces

Pickled ginger, soy sauce and additional prepared wasabi

*If you can't find white rice labeled "sushi rice", use any short grain rice.

FRIED CAULIFLOWER WITH GARLIC TAHINI SAUCE

MAKES 8 SERVINGS

1. For sauce, whisk tahini, yogurt, lemon juice, garlic and 1/4 teaspoon salt in medium bowl. Whisk in enough water in thin steady stream until sauce is thinned to desired consistency. Stir in parsley.

2. For cauliflower, whisk flour and 1/2 teaspoon salt in large bowl. Whisk eggs and 1/4 cup water in medium bowl. Combine panko, remaining 1 teaspoon salt, cumin, garlic powder and nutmeg in large bowl. Toss cauliflower florets in flour mixture to coat; tap off excess. Dip in egg mixture, letting excess drain back into bowl. Place in panko mixture; toss until coated. Place breaded cauliflower on baking sheet.

3. Line another baking sheet with three layers of paper towels. Place 3 inches of oil in large deep saucepan. Clip deep-fry or candy thermometer to side of pan. Heat over medium-high heat to 350°F; adjust heat to maintain temperature during frying. Add cauliflower in batches; cook 4 minutes or until golden brown, stirring once or twice. Drain on prepared sheet pan. Serve warm with sauce.

SAUCE

- 1/2 cup tahini
- 1/4 cup plain Greek yogurt
- 2 tablespoons lemon juice
- 2 cloves garlic, minced
- 1/4 teaspoon salt
- 6 tablespoons water
- 1 tablespoon minced fresh parsley

CAULIFLOWER

- 1 cup all-purpose flour
- 1 1/2 teaspoons salt, divided
- 4 eggs
- 1/4 cup water
- 2 cups panko bread crumbs
- 1 teaspoon ground cumin
- 1 teaspoon garlic powder
- 1/4 teaspoon ground nutmeg
- 1 large head cauliflower (2 1/2 pounds), cut into 1-inch florets

  Vegetable oil for frying

RED PEPPER ANTIPASTO

MAKES 6 TO 8 SERVINGS

1. Prepare Crostini, if desired.

2. Heat oil in large skillet over medium-high heat. Add bell peppers; cook and stir 8 to 9 minutes or until edges of peppers begin to brown. Reduce heat to medium. Add garlic; cook and stir 1 minute.

3. Add vinegar, salt and black pepper; cook 2 minutes or until liquid has evaporated. Serve warm or at room temperature with crostini, if desired.

CROSTINI: Brush thin slices of French bread with olive oil. Place on baking sheet; bake in preheated 350°F oven for 10 minutes or until golden brown.

Crostini (recipe follows, optional)

1 tablespoon olive oil

3 red bell peppers, cut into 2×1/4-inch strips

2 cloves garlic, minced

2 tablespoons red wine vinegar

1/4 teaspoon salt

Black pepper

HERBED POTATO CHIPS

MAKES 2 TO 4 SERVINGS

1. Preheat oven to 450°F. Spray two large baking sheets with nonstick cooking spray. Combine dill, garlic salt and pepper in small bowl; set aside.

2. Cut potatoes crosswise into very thin slices, about $1/16$ inch thick. Pat dry with paper towels. Arrange potato slices in single layer on prepared baking sheets; brush with 1 tablespoon oil and sprinkle lightly with salt.

3. Bake 10 minutes; turn slices over. Brush with remaining 1 tablespoon oil; sprinkle evenly with seasoning mixture.

4. Bake 5 to 10 minutes or until golden brown. Cool completely on baking sheets.

2 tablespoons minced fresh dill, thyme or rosemary or 2 teaspoons dried dill weed, thyme or rosemary

$1/4$ teaspoon garlic salt

$1/8$ teaspoon black pepper

2 peeled medium red potatoes (about 8 ounces)

2 tablespoons olive oil, divided

Salt

TOFU SATAY WITH PEANUT SAUCE

MAKES 4 SERVINGS

1. Cut tofu into 24 cubes. Combine water, soy sauce, oil, garlic and ginger in small bowl. Place tofu, mushrooms and bell pepper in large resealable food storage bag. Add soy sauce mixture; seal bag and turn gently to coat. Marinate 30 minutes, turning occasionally. Soak eight 8-inch bamboo skewers in water 20 minutes.

2. Preheat oven to 400°F. Spray 13×9-inch glass baking dish with nonstick cooking spray.

3. Drain tofu mixture; discard marinade. Thread tofu, mushrooms and bell pepper on skewers. Place skewers in prepared dish.

4. Bake 25 minutes or until tofu cubes are lightly browned and vegetables are softened.

5. Meanwhile for sauce, whisk coconut milk, peanut butter, brown sugar, vinegar and curry paste in small saucepan over medium heat. Bring to a boil, stirring constantly. Immediately reduce heat to low; cook about 20 minutes or until creamy and thick, stirring frequently. Serve satay with sauce.

TIP: To press tofu, wrap it in a double layer of paper towels and place it on a cutting board. Place another cutting board on top of it and weigh it down with cans or other sturdy, heavy objects. Let it stand for at least 30 minutes.

SATAY

- 1 package (14 to 16 ounces) firm tofu, drained and pressed (see Tip)
- 1/3 cup water
- 1/3 cup soy sauce
- 1 tablespoon toasted sesame oil
- 1 teaspoon minced garlic
- 1 teaspoon minced fresh ginger
- 16 white mushrooms, trimmed
- 1 large red bell pepper, cut into 8 pieces

PEANUT SAUCE

- 1 can (14 ounces) unsweetened coconut milk
- 1/2 cup creamy peanut butter
- 2 tablespoons packed brown sugar
- 1 tablespoon rice vinegar
- 1 to 2 teaspoons Thai red curry paste

TEXAS CAVIAR

MAKES ABOUT 9 CUPS

1. Heat canola oil in large skillet over high heat. Add corn; cook and stir about 3 minutes or until corn is beginning to brown in spots. Place in large bowl. Add black-eyed peas, beans, tomatoes, bell pepper, onion, jalapeño pepper, green onions and cilantro.

2. Combine vinegar, 1 tablespoon lime juice, salt, sugar, cumin, oregano and garlic in small bowl. Whisk in olive oil in thin steady stream until well blended. Pour over vegetables; stir to coat.

3. Refrigerate at least 2 hours or overnight. Just before serving, stir in remaining 1 teaspoon lime juice. Taste and adjust seasonings.

NOTE: For black-eyed peas, use 2 (15-ounce) cans, rinsed and drained or cook the beans from dried. Soak 8 ounces of dried beans in salted water at least 4 hours or overnight. Drain beans and place in large saucepan. Cover with water and bring to a boil over high heat. Reduce heat; simmer 45 minutes to 1 hour or until beans are tender. Drain and let cool before using.

1 tablespoon canola oil

1 cup fresh corn

3 cups cooked black-eyed peas (see Note)

1 can (about 15 ounces) black beans

1 cup halved grape tomatoes

1 bell pepper (any color), finely chopped

1/2 cup finely chopped red onion

1 jalapeño pepper, seeded and minced

2 green onions, minced

1/4 cup chopped fresh cilantro

2 tablespoons red wine vinegar

1 tablespoon plus 1 teaspoon lime juice, divided

1 teaspoon salt

1 teaspoon sugar

1/2 teaspoon ground cumin

1/2 teaspoon dried oregano

2 cloves garlic, minced

1/4 cup olive oil

BEANS AND GREENS CROSTINI

MAKES ABOUT 24 CROSTINI

1. Heat 1 tablespoon oil in large skillet over medium heat. Add onion; cook and stir 5 minutes or until softened. Add kale and 1 tablespoon garlic; cook 15 minutes or until kale is softened and most of liquid has evaporated, stirring occasionally. Stir in vinegar, 1 teaspoon salt and red pepper flakes.

2. Meanwhile, combine beans, remaining 3 tablespoons oil, 1 tablespoon garlic, 1 teaspoon salt and rosemary in food processor or blender; process until smooth.

3. Spread baguette slices with bean mixture; top with kale.

4 tablespoons olive oil, divided

1 small onion, thinly sliced

4 cups thinly sliced Italian black kale or other dinosaur kale variety

2 tablespoons minced garlic, divided

1 tablespoon balsamic vinegar

2 teaspoons salt, divided

1/4 teaspoon red pepper flakes

1 can (about 15 ounces) cannellini beans, rinsed and drained

1 tablespoon chopped fresh rosemary

Toasted baguette slices

CRISP OATS TRAIL MIX

MAKES 2$\frac{1}{2}$ CUPS (ABOUT 10 SERVINGS)

1. Preheat oven to 325°F. Line baking sheet with foil.

2. Combine all ingredients in large bowl; mix well. Spread on prepared baking sheet.

3. Bake 20 minutes or until oats are lightly browned, stirring halfway through cooking time. Cool completely on baking sheet. Store in airtight container.

1 cup old-fashioned oats

$\frac{1}{2}$ cup pepitas (raw pumpkin seeds)

$\frac{1}{2}$ cup dried sweetened cranberries

$\frac{1}{2}$ cup raisins

2 tablespoons maple syrup

1 teaspoon canola oil

$\frac{1}{2}$ teaspoon ground cinnamon

$\frac{1}{4}$ teaspoon salt

VEGETARIAN SUMMER ROLLS

MAKES 12 SUMMER ROLLS

1. Cut tofu crosswise into two pieces, each about 1 inch thick. Arrange between paper-towel lined cutting boards. Place weighted saucepan or baking dish on top; let stand 30 minutes to drain.

2. Place rice noodles in medium bowl; cover with hot water. Soak 20 to 30 minutes or until softened. Drain and cut into 3-inch lengths.

3. Meanwhile for dipping sauce, combine 1/4 cup soy sauce, lime juice, sugar, garlic and vinegar in small bowl. Stir until sugar is dissolved. Set aside.

4. Cut tofu into narrow strips about 1/4 inch thick. Place in medium bowl with remaining 1/4 cup soy sauce and sesame oil; toss gently. Heat vegetable oil in large skillet over medium heat. Add tofu and mushrooms; cook and stir until browned. Sprinkle with sesame seeds.

5. Soften rice paper wrappers, one at a time, in bowl of warm water 20 to 30 seconds. Remove and place on flat surface lined with dish towel. Arrange mint leaves in center of wrapper. Layer with tofu, mushrooms, carrots, noodles and bell pepper.

6. Fold bottom of wrapper up over filling; fold in each side and roll up. Repeat with remaining wrappers. Wrap finished rolls individually in plastic wrap or cover with damp towel until ready to serve to prevent drying out. Serve with dipping sauce.

1 package (14 to 16 ounces) firm tofu

3½ ounces thin rice noodles (rice vermicelli)

1/2 cup soy sauce, divided

2 tablespoons lime juice

1 tablespoon sugar

2 cloves garlic, crushed

1 teaspoon rice vinegar

1 teaspoon toasted sesame oil

1 tablespoon vegetable oil

2 medium portobello mushrooms, cut into thin strips

1 tablespoon sesame seeds

12 rice paper wrappers*

1 bunch fresh mint

1/2 cup shredded carrots

1 yellow bell pepper, cut into thin strips

*Rice paper is a thin, edible wrapper used in Southeast Asian cooking. It is available in the Asian aisle of the grocery store.

FRUIT DESSERTS

COCONUT AND PEANUT BUTTER QUINOA BALLS

MAKES 24 BALLS

1. Place quinoa in fine-mesh strainer; rinse well under cold running water.

2. Combine 1 cup water and quinoa in medium saucepan; bring to a boil over high heat. Reduce heat to low; cover and simmer 10 to 15 minutes or until quinoa is tender and water is absorbed. Cool slightly.

3. Meanwhile, spread coconut in large skillet. Cook over medium heat 7 to 10 minutes or until lightly brown and toasted, stirring frequently. Cool slightly.

4. Combine quinoa, 1¼ cups coconut, peanut butter, maple syrup, cinnamon and vanilla in medium bowl.

5. Shape mixture into 1-inch balls. Roll in remaining ¾ cup coconut to coat. Store in refrigerator.

½ cup uncooked quinoa

1 cup water

2 cups sweetened flaked coconut (about ½ of 14-ounce package), divided

½ cup creamy peanut butter

2 tablespoons maple syrup

½ teaspoon ground cinnamon

½ teaspoon vanilla

MAPLE-OATMEAL COOKIES

MAKES ABOUT 2 DOZEN COOKIES

1. Preheat oven to 375°F. Line cookie sheets with parchment paper. Combine oats, flour, baking soda, cinnamon and salt in medium bowl.

2. Beat butter, brown sugar and maple syrup in large bowl with electric mixer at medium speed 1 minute or until creamy. Gradually beat in flour mixture just until blended. Beat in raisins.

3. Drop batter by heaping tablespoonfuls 1 inch apart onto prepared cookie sheets. Flatten slightly.

4. Bake 13 to 16 minutes or until golden. Cool on cookie sheets 5 minutes; remove to wire racks. Serve warm.

$1\frac{1}{2}$ **cups old-fashioned oats**

$\frac{3}{4}$ **cup all-purpose flour**

$\frac{1}{2}$ **teaspoon baking soda**

$\frac{1}{2}$ **teaspoon ground cinnamon**

$\frac{1}{4}$ **teaspoon salt**

$\frac{1}{2}$ **cup (1 stick) vegan plant butter or regular butter, softened**

$\frac{1}{2}$ **cup packed brown sugar or palm sugar**

$\frac{1}{2}$ **cup maple syrup**

$\frac{1}{2}$ **cup raisins**

BLUEBERRY-PEAR TART

MAKES 8 SERVINGS

1. For pie pastry, combine flour and salt in medium bowl. Cut in butter with pastry blender or fingers until mixture resembles coarse crumbs. Combine 3 tablespoons ice water and vinegar in small bowl. Sprinkle over flour mixture while mixing with fork until dough forms, adding additional water as needed. Shape dough into a disc; wrap in plastic wrap. Refrigerate 30 minutes.

2. Preheat oven to 450°F.

3. Spray 9-inch tart pan with nonstick cooking spray. Roll out pie pastry into 11-inch circle on lightly floured surface. Place in pan; press against side of pan to form 1/2-inch edge. Trim edge. Prick dough several times with fork. Bake 12 minutes. Cool completely in pan on wire rack.

4. Arrange pear slices on bottom of cooled crust; top with blueberries.

5. Place fruit spread in small microwavable bowl; cover with plastic wrap. Microwave on HIGH 15 seconds; stir. Repeat, if necessary, until spread is melted. Stir in ginger until blended. Let stand 30 seconds to thicken slightly. Pour over fruit in crust. Refrigerate 2 hours before serving. (Do not cover.)

1 1/4 cups all-purpose flour

1/2 teaspoon salt

6 tablespoons cold vegan plant butter or regular butter, cut into pieces

3 to 4 tablespoons ice water

1/2 teaspoon cider vinegar

1 medium ripe pear, peeled and thinly sliced

8 ounces fresh or thawed frozen blueberries or blackberries

1/3 cup raspberry fruit spread

1/2 teaspoon grated fresh ginger

APPLE CRANBERRY CRUMBLE

MAKES 4 SERVINGS

1. Preheat oven to 375°F.

2. Combine apples, cranberries, granulated sugar, 2 tablespoons flour, $1/2$ teaspoon apple pie spice and $1/8$ teaspoon salt in large bowl; toss to coat. Spoon into medium (8-inch) cast iron skillet.

3. Combine remaining 4 tablespoons flour, walnuts, oats, brown sugar, remaining $1/2$ teaspoon apple pie spice and $1/8$ teaspoon salt in medium bowl; mix well. Cut in butter with pastry blender or fingers until mixture resembles coarse crumbs. Sprinkle over fruit mixture in skillet.

4. Bake 50 to 60 minutes or until filling is bubbly and topping is lightly browned.

4 large apples (about $1^1/3$ pounds), peeled and cut into $1/4$-inch slices

2 cups fresh or frozen cranberries

$1/3$ cup granulated sugar

6 tablespoons all-purpose flour, divided

1 teaspoon apple pie spice, divided

$1/4$ teaspoon salt, divided

$1/2$ cup chopped walnuts

$1/4$ cup old-fashioned oats

2 tablespoons packed brown sugar

$1/4$ cup ($1/2$ stick) cold vegan plant butter or regular butter, cut into small pieces

CHOCOLATE DRIZZLED GRAPE SKEWERS

MAKES 6 SERVINGS

1. Wash grapes; remove stems. Dry completely with paper towel. Thread grapes on skewers. Line rimmed baking sheet with waxed paper. Place skewers on baking sheet with ends resting on the rim.

2. Place semisweet chocolate chips in small microwavable bowl; microwave on HIGH 1 minute. Stir. Microwave at 30-second intervals, stirring after each interval until smooth. Drizzle over grapes, rotating skewers for even coverage.

3. Place white chocolate chips in separate small microwavable bowl; microwave on HIGH 1 minute. Stir. Microwave at 30-second intervals, stirring after each interval until smooth. Drizzle over grapes, rotating skewers for even coverage.

4. Freeze 2 hours before serving.

2 cups seedless grapes (green, red or a combination)

$1/4$ cup semisweet chocolate chips

$1/4$ cup white chocolate chips

OATMEAL APRICOT GINGER COOKIES

MAKES 2 DOZEN COOKIES

1. Preheat oven to 375°F. Line cookie sheets with parchment paper. Combine boiling water and flaxseed in small bowl. Refrigerate until cold.

2. Beat granulated sugar, brown sugar, butter and oil in large bowl with electric mixer at medium speed 3 minutes or until light and fluffy. Add flaxseed mixture, ginger, baking soda and salt; beat until well blended. Add oats and flour; mix on low speed until well blended. Stir in apricots. Drop dough by tablespoonfuls 2 inches apart onto prepared cookie sheets (6 cookies per sheet).

3. Bake about 8 minutes or until slightly golden on edges and light in the middle. (Cookies will not look done but will continue to cook while cooling.) Cool on cookie sheets 3 minutes. Remove to wire racks; cool completely.

3 tablespoons boiling water

1 tablespoon ground flaxseed

1/2 cup granulated sugar

1/4 cup packed brown sugar

1/4 cup (1/2 stick) vegan plant butter or regular butter, softened

2 tablespoons vegetable oil

1 1/2 teaspoons ground ginger

3/4 teaspoon baking soda

1/2 teaspoon salt

1 1/4 cups old-fashioned oats

1/2 cup all-purpose flour

6 ounces whole dried apricots, chopped

METRIC CONVERSION CHART

VOLUME MEASUREMENTS (dry)

$1/8$ teaspoon = 0.5 mL
$1/4$ teaspoon = 1 mL
$1/2$ teaspoon = 2 mL
$3/4$ teaspoon = 4 mL
1 teaspoon = 5 mL
1 tablespoon = 15 mL
2 tablespoons = 30 mL
$1/4$ cup = 60 mL
$1/3$ cup = 75 mL
$1/2$ cup = 125 mL
$2/3$ cup = 150 mL
$3/4$ cup = 175 mL
1 cup = 250 mL
2 cups = 1 pint = 500 mL
3 cups = 750 mL
4 cups = 1 quart = 1 L

VOLUME MEASUREMENTS (fluid)

1 fluid ounce (2 tablespoons) = 30 mL
4 fluid ounces ($1/2$ cup) = 125 mL
8 fluid ounces (1 cup) = 250 mL
12 fluid ounces ($1 1/2$ cups) = 375 mL
16 fluid ounces (2 cups) = 500 mL

WEIGHTS (mass)

$1/2$ ounce = 15 g
1 ounce = 30 g
3 ounces = 90 g
4 ounces = 120 g
8 ounces = 225 g
10 ounces = 285 g
12 ounces = 360 g
16 ounces = 1 pound = 450 g

DIMENSIONS

$1/16$ inch = 2 mm
$1/8$ inch = 3 mm
$1/4$ inch = 6 mm
$1/2$ inch = 1.5 cm
$3/4$ inch = 2 cm
1 inch = 2.5 cm

OVEN TEMPERATURES

250°F = 120°C
275°F = 140°C
300°F = 150°C
325°F = 160°C
350°F = 180°C
375°F = 190°C
400°F = 200°C
425°F = 220°C
450°F = 230°C

BAKING PAN SIZES

Utensil	Size in Inches/Quarts	Metric Volume	Size in Centimeters
Baking or Cake Pan (square or rectangular)	8×8×2	2 L	20×20×5
	9×9×2	2.5 L	23×23×5
	12×8×2	3 L	30×20×5
	13×9×2	3.5 L	33×23×5
Loaf Pan	8×4×3	1.5 L	20×10×7
	9×5×3	2 L	23×13×7
Round Layer Cake Pan	8×1½	1.2 L	20×4
	9×1½	1.5 L	23×4
Pie Plate	8×1¼	750 mL	20×3
	9×1¼	1 L	23×3
Baking Dish or Casserole	1 quart	1 L	—
	1½ quart	1.5 L	—
	2 quart	2 L	—